Proclamation 4

Aids for Interpreting
the Lessons of the Church Year

Epiphany

D1710355

Frederick Houk Borsch

ı٦

Series A

FORTRESS PRESS   **MINNEAPOLIS**

PROCLAMATION 4
Aids for Interpreting the Lessons of the Church Year
Series A: Epiphany

Biblical quotations, unless otherwise noted, are from the Revised Standard Version of the Bible, copyright © 1946, 1952, and 1971 by the Division of Christian Education of the National Council of Churches.

Library of Congress Cataloging-in-Publication Data

(Revised for vol. 1–3, Series A)

Proclamation 4.

  Consists of 24 volumes in 3 series designated A, B, and C, which correspond to the cycles of the three year lectionary. Each series contains 8 basic volumes with the following titles: [1] Advent-Christmas, [2] Epiphany, [3] Lent, [4] Holy Week, [5] Easter, [6] Pentecost 1, [7] Pentecost 2, and [8] Pentecost 3. (In addition there are four volumes on the lesser festivals.)
  By Christopher R. Seitz and others.
  Includes bibliographies.
  1. Bible—Liturgical lessons, English. 2. Bible—Homiletical use. 3. Bible—Criticism, interpretation, etc. 4. Common lectionary. 5. Church year. I. Seitz, Christopher R. II. Title: Proclamation four.
BS391.2.S37 1988   264'.34   88–10982
ISBN 0-8006-4162-0 (Series A, Epiphany).

Manufactured in the U.S.A.   AF 1–4162

93   92   91   90   89   1   2   3   4   5   6   7   8   9   10

Contents

The Epiphany of Our Lord   5

The Baptism of Our Lord
The First Sunday after the Epiphany   10

The Second Sunday after the Epiphany   16

The Third Sunday after the Epiphany   23

The Fourth Sunday after the Epiphany   29

The Fifth Sunday after the Epiphany   35

The Sixth Sunday after the Epiphany   40

The Seventh Sunday after the Epiphany   47

The Eighth Sunday after the Epiphany   53

The Transfiguration of Our Lord
The Last Sunday after the Epiphany   59

The Epiphany of Our Lord

Lutheran	Roman Catholic	Episcopal	Common Lectionary
Isa. 60:1–6	Isa. 60:1–6	Isa. 60:1–6,9	Isa. 60:1–6
Eph. 3:2–12	Eph. 3:2–3a, 5–6	Eph. 3:1–12	Eph. 3:1–12
Matt. 2:1–12	Matt. 2:1–12	Matt. 2:1–12	Matt. 2:1–12

Perhaps the most persistent of human dreams is that we are not alone in the cosmos. We hope that life and what happens to us are not an accident to which the universe is indifferent. In modern dress, expressions of this yearning sometimes take the form of stories about visitors from outer space or UFO sightings. In every age versions of astrology have offered the comfort that there is some design. Our lessons powerfully speak from a theistic faith to this longing. They tell of God's means of salvation and symbolically or explicitly picture the extension of this salvation beyond Judaism to the Gentile world. Light and revelation transform darkness and hiddenness.

Christians are called to respond by proclaiming "the unsearchable riches of Christ" (Eph. 3:8) and by becoming missionaries, but the very first response is simply awe, joy, and then the worshipful bringing of gifts by the nations and by the Magi. In their different ways, however, the readings emphasize not human action and certainly not human initiative, but what God does to dispel darkness and the fear that there is no purpose or redemption for life. "The gift of God's grace" (Eph. 3:7) is in each case sudden and surprising in character. The wise men behold the star and the promised child. The people of Jerusalem lift up their eyes and see by the new light of God their sons and daughters returning and the nations coming bearing their gifts. To Paul and his readers God's purpose has been revealed "to enlighten everyone" (Eph. 3:9) with the plan for the salvation of all. The three lessons each tell of a "manifestation" or "appearing" (= epiphany, literally "shining upon") of God's grace and the "throbbing and enlarging of the heart" (Isa. 60:5), "exceeding great joy" (Matt. 2:10), new "freedom (or "boldness")" and confidence" (Eph. 3:12) in the relationship with God.

FIRST LESSON: ISAIAH 60:1–6

The three passages suggest or make specific reference to historical time and event, while they also allude to the cosmic scale and that which transcends the historical plane. Isaiah 60—62 has a number of characteristics in common with the earlier chapters of this book ascribed to Second Isaiah (40—55), but may have been composed in a slightly later period. At this time some, but by no means all, of the Judean people have returned from exile in Babylon. A more settled life has been restored in Jerusalem, but its inhabitants do not know prosperity and are conscious of those who are still in exile. God's plan of salvation is not yet complete, and the prophet pictures that new day which may be said to stand at the edge or even just beyond human history. The vision can be seen as the beginning of eschatology in Israelite prophecy—a peering beyond fulfillment *in* history to the fulfillment *of* history.

The prophet (or, as often through this section, the Lord through the prophet) speaks to the city, addressing her as feminine. The double imperative is characteristic of the style of Second Isaiah. The prophetic vision projects its hearers through a time and tense in which darkness will continue to cover the land and people to a future which, in the vision, "has come." The Lord is alluded to as the sun—imagery frequently used of God in other religions and sometimes in Israel, where, however, God is never confused with the sun. In the imagery there may be a memory (if not awareness of a continuing practice) of imagining the Lord God coming to Jerusalem like the sun rising over the Mount of Olives and radiating on the temple—perhaps into the temple itself. Jerusalem shines forth, reflecting God's glory. The word for glory, *kabôth* (in its root meanings suggestive of "weight," "importance," even "opulence") has a rich biblical heritage as a way of speaking of the Lord's presence, especially in relation to worship and the cultus.

The new light of the city causes the nations to come to Jerusalem bringing the children of the exile and also, by sea and by land, bringing wealth that will be used in God's praise. Verse 4 is virtually a quotation of the prophecy of Isa. 49:18, 22. The references to Midian, Ephah, and Sheba in v. 6 nicely pick up Gen. 25:3–4, for these peoples also are descendants of Abraham, now come to Jerusalem for the praise of the Lord.

GOSPEL: MATTHEW 2:1–12

In the imagery and tones of another time and story Matthew develops many of the same themes. Although later embellishment tells us that there were three Magi (deduced from the three gifts) and that they were kings and definitely Gentiles, the men (sages, wise men who sought insights into the natural world and its secrets) are fairly clearly foreigners who have come to Jerusalem to worship. Psalm 72 (the proper liturgical psalm for the Epiphany) also may have played a part in the background with its references to foreign kings bringing gifts to God's king in Israel. One of those gifts is gold (Ps. 72:15). Gold and frankincense are brought for the Lord's praise in Isa. 60:6. Myrrh is a royal fragrance in Ps. 45:8.

It is not, however, the child "born king of the Jews" that the Magi first encounter. It is another king, a man who had fought his way to the top in Palestine and clung to his throne with the help of the Romans for thirty-three years. Although he had relatives put to death and committed other ruthless acts, Herod also had many accomplishments to his credit and was not necessarily more cruel than other rulers of the time. We have no other record of his having ordered all male children under two years of age to be put to death, but such an act would not have been inconsistent with the character of a king insecure in his old age in a land full of rumors. Probably more to the point, the evangelist is concerned with yet another typology which becomes more clear as the story develops. The child's early experience parallels that of Moses, whose young life was also threatened by a cruel king. Hearers of Matthew's story begin to understand that this child is to be the new prophet, as Moses promised in Scripture (Deut. 18:15).

The Christian pilgrim who goes to the Holy Land today also first encounters Herod rather than Jesus. As one is guided about from south to north, viewing Masada, the Herodium, ancient portions of the temple platform in Jerusalem, to Caesarea, and all the way up to Caesarea Philippi, one finds remains of Herod's activity, but none of Jesus'. In a sense, pilgrims have to search like the Magi to find Jesus. Even when they arrive at the churches built in his honor, pilgrims still may feel unsure that they have come close to Jesus. Perhaps only when one worships with his followers, breaks bread, tells his stories, and tries to alleviate some of the suffering in that land is the living spirit of Jesus found.

Many Christians first hear this Gospel passage in the context of a pageant, very likely enacted by children in bathrobes and cardboard crowns. As I watch such pageants, musing on my own reactions, I also wonder what is going through the minds of the audience and the child actors. What inklings of incongruity and irony they all must feel while watching such an awesome and terrifying story being played out amid the somber choir pews. Yet somehow the relative innocence and youthful awe of the children also make the themes of searching hope against conniving evil, of acts of humble worship outwitting worldly power, seem more credible in retelling a story in which the central figure, through whom God's purpose of salvation is to be accomplished, is a helpless infant.

I wonder, too, at how the young people are chosen for their parts. Since there is only one role clearly marked for a girl, and that an exalted one, I imagine her to be a standout of some kind in her class. Though not spoken of in this passage, Joseph is always there, the young actor seeming to be chosen for his docility. The Magi are probably the best roles. They are able to move about, bear the Christmas-present-like boxes, outfox Herod, and depart to their own country "by another way" (out the door to the sacristy?).

I always wonder the most about Herod. Who wants to play King Herod? It may be my imagination, but the boy usually seems a bit larger and perhaps fatter than the others. But rather than being a bully, he seems like someone others pick on, maybe a little dull behind his glued-on mustache. Perhaps that is how they get him to play the part, for probably no hearers of the story want to identify with King Herod. Yet in several ways it may be the part that needs the most attention, and the preacher might help those in the congregation recognize that the story cannot be real if everyone just wants to play the parts of Mary, Joseph, and the Magi. There would not be slaughters of the innocents, so many babies dying of poor nutrition and lack of medical care, children given few opportunities for recreation and education, many living in dangerous slums, if the rest of us were only innocent parents and wise men, without any Herod in us.

And then there is that star—source of endless speculation. Some want to find for it a reality outside the story—perhaps in the coincidence of two stars or planets, or in a supernova. They could be right. Some such heavenly light may be remembered in the telling of the story, and it piques the imagination to consider how many light-years earlier such rays of light would have left the highest heavens to have shone on earth at this time. Talk of divine plan and cosmic significance! But that, of course, is true of the star in the story, too. The cosmic and the divine are the dimensions it brings into the narrative. There may also be a messianic allusion to Num. 24:17—"a star shall come forth out of Jacob."

In one way the star plays a rather odd role in the plot, since it does not immediately lead the Magi to Jesus' home. (In Matthew's story Bethlehem seems more the original family home than Nazareth. One also has a sense, despite our liturgical association of the story with Christmas and the birth narrative, that the evangelist may be thinking of the infant as now being one or two years old.) Only when the Magi are given the scriptural reference do they know where to go. (The passage is introduced with a formula citation ("This was to fulfill what was spoken"), which Matthew employs similarly thirteen times; and the passage is quoted with a slight inexactitude with respect to the known versions of the Jewish Scriptures, which is also typical of the evangelist.) The star now guides them with precision. The quotation of Mic. 5:2 seems to have been influenced by 2 Sam. 5:2, and establishes Matthew's conviction that the certain plan of God is to be recognized not only in nature's star but also in Scripture.

EPISTLE: EPHESIANS 3:2–12

Paul (or a later disciple seeking to convey what Paul would have written were he still living) also insists that God has a plan of salvation with both earthly and cosmic dimensions. An important word in this discussion is *oikonomia* in Eph. 3:2, 9, which can mean the plan of God's grace entrusted to Paul to proclaim and/or the stewardship Paul has been given over the revelation of God. The words "revelation" and "reveals" (*apokalypsis*, from which comes our word apocalyptic) in vv. 3 and 5 and "mystery" *(mystērion)* in vv. 3, 4, and 9 are words from the vocabulary of apocalyptic writings and refer to secrets known formerly only to God or to God and heavenly beings. In one sense these "unsearchable" (cf. the "love of Christ surpassing knowledge" of Eph. 3:19 and "the depth of the riches and wisdom and knowledge of God" of Rom 11:33) "riches of Christ" are the totality of God's plan of salvation, but more specifically this revealed mystery is the inclusion of the Gentiles as "members of the same body" of Christ (v. 6: see Rom. 12:4–8; 1 Cor. 12:4–31 on the image of the one body) that has only now been made known. The surprising aspect of this revelation from the perspective of those who were Jewish must be underscored. Jews understood themselves to have a special relationship with God which could not be shared or could only be shared as others came to worship as did the Jews. It was, therefore, astounding that God should use the Christ (the Messiah) as a means of reaching out to include Gentiles on equal terms as "companion heirs." (Moffatt's translation of v. 6 renders the three words beginning with *syn-* in Greek as "coheirs, companions, and copartners.") To Gentile Christians it must have seemed just as surprising that it was through Judaism that God was offering them salvation. One recalls the earlier image of "the dividing wall of hostility" that existed for Gentiles, "separated from Christ, alienated from the commonwealth of Israel, and strangers to the covenants of promise, having no hope and without God in the world." The reconciling work of Christ has been to bring together both Jew and Gentile by means of one common offering and sacrifice for all—"in one body through the cross." So "he is our peace" (Eph. 2:11–18).

This new, radically equal community of faith is meant to be made manifest on earth in the church. It is the "household of God, built upon the foundation of the apostles and prophets, Christ Jesus himself being the chief cornerstone" (Eph. 2:19–20). Its significance, however, reaches beyond earth into the cosmos so that God's plan and wisdom can be made known to "the principipalities and powers" (3:10). These *exsousiai* ("authorities") and *epouranioi* ("heavenly beings") were conceived of as like demigods, sometimes opposed to God's will, who functioned as the ruling conceptualities for various human expressions of authority and governance. They were now to be shown a new kind of human oneness by the church—the plan of "God who created all things" (Eph. 3:10; see Col. 1:24–27 for a closely parallel teaching).

The preacher would do well to reflect with the congregation on that exalted role and mission for the church and also on reasons why the church falls short of the goal so that dividing walls of hostility still exist, especially between Gentiles and Jews. Do Gentile Christians sometimes forget that the grace of God has made them coheirs? Does being a Christian become a matter of privilege? How can the church (and this particular congregation) live so as to embody an equality that breaks down barriers of inequalities formed by race and ethnicity ("neither Jew nor Greek"), economic class ("neither slave nor free"), and gender ("neither male nor female"; see Gal. 3:27–8) and so make *epiphanies* of God's revealed plan of salvation?

Despite all their shortcomings, Christians may hope and strive to do this because of the "boldness" or "freedom" (*parrēsia* suggests courage and willingness to speak frankly) and confidence they have in approaching God (Eph. 3:12). They have this because of what may be translated as "his faith" or "faithfulness," or as "faith in him" (meaning in Christ or God), or the phrase may suggest all these aspects—the mutuality of a trust relationship. Many people fear or do not dare to approach the Creator of all things. God's showing forth in Jesus and revelation of the inclusive plan of salvation has opened a new way of relationship with God and with one another.

The Baptism of Our Lord
The First Sunday after the Epiphany

Lutheran	Roman Catholic	Episcopal	Common Lectionary
Isa. 42:1–7	Isa. 42:1–4, 6–7	Isa. 42:1–9	Isa. 42:1–9
Acts 10:34–38	Acts 10:34–38	Acts 10:34–38	Acts 10:34–43
Matt. 3:13–17	Matt. 3:13–17	Matt. 3:13–17	Matt. 3:13–17

FIRST LESSON: ISAIAH 42:1–9
EPISTLE: ACTS 10:34–38
GOSPEL: MATTHEW 3:13–17

Whom does God choose? Why? How? For what? On this day the church's readings ask hearers to meditate on the ministry of Isaiah's servant, on the ministries of Peter, Cornelius, and Jesus, and on their own ministries. It is a time to reflect especially on the beginnings of ministries, to think about new and renewed ministries.

When I hear people despairing about their lives or life in general, frequently there is one thing in particular they mention. They may use different words, but they speak of a lack of sense of purpose, of something they can contribute, of abilities they can share with others, a ministry for their life. Perhaps the greatest gift the community of the church can give to its members is a sense of ministry, help in discerning what individuals can do singly and corporately for others, and then support in carrying out such ministries.

Most people, of course, have several ministries; for example, as parent, son or daughter, spouse, lawyer, bricklayer, teacher, or custodian, church school teacher, colleague, neighbor, friend, member of the task force for better housing for the poor. Preaching is one of the ways people may be helped to discern and better understand the several aspects of their vocation. It is also a means by which the congregation as a whole may be called to its ministry.

Who are called? Whom does God choose? While Jesus and Isaiah's servant are special figures chosen for extraordinary and decisive ministries, and in their ways Peter and Cornelius also seem almost larger-than-life figures, still it is important to remember that their importance to the ongoing community of faith derives in large measure from the fact that their ministries were carried forward amid all the trivialities, frustrations, and the ebb and flow of mortal lives. We can learn from them.

The servant is "chosen" because God's "soul" (very being) delights in him. The word translated as "delights" means "to find favor," "approve," "take pleasure in," "to associate with," and "to love." Yet when one understands the servant's mission, one recalls those somewhat querulous words of St. Theresa of Avila, "Lord, it is no wonder you have so few friends, given how you treat them."

Jesus is also "loved" (*agapētos*), paralleling the word "chosen" in Isa. 42:1 and indicating God's purpose and will more than an emotion. The phrase "with whom I am well pleased" picks up the idea of "delight" in Isaiah's words. While in Mark's parallel story of the baptism (1:9–11) it might be inferred that Jesus was chosen to be God's Son at the time of baptism (the heavenly voice addresses Jesus in the second person), Matthew clearly understands that Jesus was God's chosen one and Son (see Matt. 2:15) from birth. Thus the voice is not for Jesus but for John and others: "This is my beloved Son" or "my Son, the beloved one." In both the readings from Isaiah and Matthew the emphasis is on God's action in choosing, and loving those chosen, for a special mission.

It is probably easier for most people to associate with Cornelius. In one sense he was but one of many Gentiles who became Christians in those early days, but he is especially singled out as the first and a kind of exemplar Gentile convert. We are told he was a centurion, a Roman military officer, devout and a "God fearer," which was a way of describing some Gentiles who worshiped God as known by the Jews without taking on the laws and customs of Judaism. We hear also of his charitable acts and persistent prayer (Acts 10:1–2, 22). Acts 10:35 stresses Cornelius's "fear" (awe and reverence) of God and his ethical character. Luke wants hearers of his story of the early church to understand that anyone of such character is acceptable to God, for God "shows no partiality" (literally, "accepts no one's face") with respect to ethnicity, and so on. (This theme of "no partiality" is repeated with various purposes in Rom. 2:11, ; Eph. 6:9; Col. 3:25; 1 Pet. 1:17; see Deut. 10:17 from which it may derive; and James 2:1, 9 where Christians are likewise to be impartial.)

It may be still easier for hearers to associate themselves with Peter who here exercises his ministry as disciple and apostle, for one recalls his mundane background and impulsive, wavering ways. But, evidently sustained by the Lord's persistent calling to him, Peter has persevered, and Luke wants hearers to recognize that it was Peter, not Paul, through whom the Spirit began the mission to the Gentiles.

While Jesus must always be exceptional for us, the lessons teach that those whom the Lord calls to ministry will come from different backgrounds and may or may not be remarkable people by the world's standards. The ministries of these servants and disciples come dramatically through a prophetic voice, a voice from heaven, angels, and dream visions. What they share in common is the action of God's Spirit (Isa. 42:1; Matt. 3:16; Acts 10:38, 44–47). Although many disciples do not experience such definitive callings, they yet have the dramatic character of their baptismal rite to recall and renew. Therein they are called upon to renounce the ways of evil, to seek to follow in the way of Jesus, to proclaim the good news of God in Christ by word and example, and to "strive for justice and peace among all people" (*Book of Common Prayer,* p. 305 and similarly in other traditions).

The word "justice" stands out in the passage from Isaiah, occurring three times in the first four verses. The Hebrew word *mishpaṭ* has nuances that are difficult to catch in a single English word. It is, first of all, more particular and active in meaning than an abstract or ideal conception of justice. It is the making and doing of just acts, defending the rights of another. In some contexts it is more juridical, meaning "judgment," but here, in associating with *torah* ("law," "way of God") it suggests teaching or instructions of justice—at least as much by deed and example as by word.

In v. 7 this mission is given further definition: it is "to open the eyes that are blind, to bring out the prisoners from the dungeon, from the prison those who sit in darkness." These words should in one sense be taken literally, for there is a ministry to the blind and to prisoners, but the significance also extends to bringing the meaning of justice to all who cannot see it and freeing people from all manner of darkness and oppression. It means bringing forth from the prison's darkness not only the captives but the jailers who must live in prisons too.

In what has been called his inaugural sermon (Luke 4:18–19) Jesus reads Isa. 61:1 with wording very similar to Isa. 42:1b, 7. His proclamation of "the good news to the poor," like the ministry of Isaiah's servant, also signifies new sight and liberty for the captives and the oppressed. The preaching of the kingdom of God means that God's demand for righteousness and acts of rendering judgment and justice are even now making themselves known in the world.

The Acts reading summarizes this ministry, telling how Jesus preached the good news throughout Judea and "went about doing good and healing all that were oppressed by the devil" (Acts 10:37–38). Furthermore, we hear that the message is "good news of peace" with all the rich associations of the word peace in the Bible, suggesting harmony, full relationship, and reconciliation between God and humanity and among all peoples. Cornelius, "one who fears God and does what is right" is clearly now meant to follow Peter in preaching the good news of and about Jesus and extolling God. In like manner every disciple can be asked how they may share the good news in their lives. While it is appropriate to talk about "varieties of service" and "gifts that differ" (1 Corinthians 4—5; Rom. 12:6), there is also a common ministry and one Spirit. The ministry of all Christians is, by word and deed, to share God's good news and to work for justice and the making of peace.

This message and ministry is to reach out to all. One does not know how the author of Isaiah 40—55 (and particularly the so-called servant songs, Isa. 42:1–4; 49:1–6; 50:4–11; 52:13—53:12—sometimes divided differently and to which 42:5–9 and 49:7–13 are sometimes added) caught his vision of the servant's ministry to the nations. While not unique in Jewish Scriptures, a ministry to the nations is unusual and particularly remarkable at a time when the people of Judah were so beleaguered— whether having returned to Jerusalem or still in exile. Our question is related to the unsolved issue as to whether Second Isaiah conceived the servant as an individual (whether himself or another prophet) or as the whole people of God or a remnant thereof. Perhaps in some sense the servant is both a representative individual (so for Christians foreshadowing Jesus) and the people. The preacher might use this representative and corporate character as a way of reflecting on both particular and representative ministries within the congregation and the work of the congregation and the church as a whole.

Perhaps the prophet's experience with the exile made him think of ways in which Israel's mission was to reach out—to be a beacon "light" of justice and liberty to the nations and a covenant (*berith,* either through a sharing of Israel's covenant laws or through a new universal covenant, with all this word's associations of God's relationship of fidelity) to all people. This spirit of universalism is given a theological foundation in the lyrical characterization of God as creator of the heavens and earth and inspiration of all people in v. 5.

Jesus' ministry, though perhaps originally conceived of as preparing only Israel for God's reign (through which people the light would then beckon to other nations), evidently even in his lifetime began to attract and reach out to non-Jews. After his resurrection his message and the message about him could not be contained in one religion. Christians today need to remind themselves of how surprising and problematic were this surge of the Spirit and the urge to proclaim the faith of Jesus to others.

Luke uses the story of the angelic vision to Cornelius, Peter's dream and proclamation to Cornelius along with his relatives and friends, and the coming of the Holy Spirit upon them in Acts 10 (a story repeated for emphasis in Acts 11:5–17) as an example and conclusive argument for what God has willed for the church. Peter's speech is meant as a classic illustration of the character of the basic Christian proclamation with its summary of Jesus' ministry, death and new life, apostolic witness, reference to scriptural warrant and proof, and offer of the forgiveness of sins. The lineaments of the Apostles' Creed can be discerned in this sample sermon.

Another characteristic that is particularly evident in the ministry of both the servant and Jesus is their humility and lowliness. Indeed, it has often been thought that Jesus was strongly influenced by Isaiah's servant. At the least, it is clear that the disciples came to see the fulfillment of this prophetic vision in him. At several points the basic kerygma refers to Jesus as the servant (*pais;* Acts 3:12, 26; 4:27, 30) with clear allusion to the Isaianic figure, and Jesus at crucial junctures in his ministry describes his own servant ministry and that of his disciples (particularly, Mark 9:35–37; 10:42–45, using *diakonos),* speaks of the blessedness of the meek, merciful, and poor in spirit (Matt. 5:3, 5, 7), and of how the humble shall be exalted (Luke 14:11 and parallels).

The servant of Isa. 42:1–9 seems in some ways a royal figure, called to render judgment and justice, and in others a prophet, a proclaimer of

justice and teacher of the law. What is unusual is his gentleness. He will
not set forth justice by having the law loudly proclaimed as a new king
might. In subtle imagery, with a touch of mystery to it, he will not even
break a bruised reed or an already dimly burning wick. (There is poetry
in the repetition of words in vv. 3–4, difficult to render into English: *bruised
reed, dimly burning wick,* bring forth *justice*/he will not *burn dimly,* be
bruised, until he has established *justice.*) One perceives in the song a figure
with both the strength of endurance and conviction, given by God's mission
and Spirit, and a tenderness toward those whom the dictates of justice and
judgment might otherwise destroy.

Usually when one hears talk about leadership, there is much reference
to the need for strength. A strong leader! Perhaps too often leaders or
would-be leaders show their strength against the weak—the bruised reeds
and dimly burning wicks. Their statements about justice are more often
rhetoric and slogans than sight for the blind and liberty for captives.

Thinking of Isaiah's servant, I recall Jesus' words about being "wise as
serpents and innocent as doves" (Matt. 10:16), which Martin Luther King,
Jr., in commenting on the meaning of true strength, took to mean that
disciples were to be strong of mind and will but tender of heart, especially
to the less fortunate. Sadly, the world does not often value, even while in
another sense it longs for, those who will lead, not by means of violence
and coercion, but by true justice and servanthood. Isaiah and Matthew tell
of the inauguration of such servants, and Peter's speech summarizes the
ministry of the servant Messiah.

Since the third century the Orthodox churches of the East have used the
story of Jesus' baptism as the Gospel reading for the Epiphany. For them
it is the first of Jesus' epiphanies or manifestations of who he is for all
humanity. Along with Easter and Pentecost the Epiphany has for them
ranked as a chief feast of the church. In a sense it replaces Christmas for
the Orthodox, offering its distinctive conception of the one proclaimed to
be God's Son in human life. Particularly interesting in this regard is the
conversation between Jesus and John, perhaps supplied by the evangelist
or his tradition to deal with the double problem of why Jesus would need
to be baptized by one whom he superseded (see Matt. 3:11) for a baptism
for the remission of sins. The answer is found in Jesus' words, "For thus
it is fitting for us to fulfill all righteousness" (3:15), suggesting a willingness
to be counted with the sinful humanity God wants to redeem. He fully
identifies with the people Israel whom God in Scripture calls "son" (Hos.
11:1). In one sense it is as the representative of this people (in his humanity
as the obedient one who reflects the character of his divine parent) that
the voice calls Jesus "son" in this passage. Matthew, always conscious of
typology, wants the hearers of his Gospel to think of Jesus as the true

Israel, passing through the waters of baptism in a new exodus, beginning a new covenant with God.

The waters of exodus and baptism are capable of drowning as well as purifying and giving life. This polyvalence allows the association of the baptism with Jesus' death and resurrection (see Mark 10:39; Rom. 6:3–11) and the dying and rising experience of disciples at baptism. It may also hark back to the water ordeals of ancient kings (still remembered in a number of the Psalms; e.g., 69:1–3) before their enthronements, and so help one understand how a story about an individual's baptism reads more like an inauguration to an anointed role. Awareness of this background in royal ritual deepens the sense in which Jesus is here God's son. The descending of the dove would probably have caused hearers of the time to think as well of the Spirit of God hovering over the face of the waters in Gen. 1:1. This then is a new time of creation and of a new humanity that God has called his son. So rich a story certainly deserves its place at the beginning of Epiphany.

The Second Sunday after the Epiphany

Lutheran	Roman Catholic	Episcopal	Common Lectionary
Isa. 49:1–6	Isa. 49:3, 5–6	Isa. 49:1–7	Isa. 49:1–7
1 Cor. 1:1–9	1 Cor. 1:1–3	1 Cor. 1:1–9	1 Cor. 1:1–9
John 1:29–41	John 1:29–34	John 1:29–41	John 1:29–34

Witnessing to God's purposes is often far from easy. There can be difficulty in understanding God's will. That will may go beyond or even in a different direction from the expectations of one's religious community. Each individual and group also has to deal with mixed motives and desires for some measure of self-glorification. Moreover, in the eyes of the world, and often in one's own perception as well, what is being accomplished in God's name may well seem insignificant. We may talk and preach at length about manifesting God and God's mighty acts to all peoples during the Epiphany season, but one also experiences frustration, questioning, and the necessity of dealing with all the niggling details of life. Trying to be a prophet and servant of God can be lonely and sometimes disheartening.

We do not know what led the one speaking as the servant of the Lord to say, "I have labored in vain, I have spent my strength for nothing (*tōhu* can refer to a desert wilderness; see also the void of creation of Gen. 1:2; Jer. 4:23) and vanity" (Isa. 49:4). One recalls the laments of Jeremiah and all of Moses' ups and downs. Despite the upbeat tone of the opening of Paul's First Letter to the Corinthians, we know he had frustrating disputes with them, even including a misunderstanding about a proposed visit (see 2 Cor. 1:15—2:4). While the testimony of John the Baptist is forthright in today's Gospel lesson, the Gospels of Matthew (11:2–3) and Luke (7:18–19) suggest a time when John may have been less certain. Behind the Fourth Gospel's account of how John's disciples came to follow Jesus may lie a more complex human story.

FIRST LESSON: ISAIAH 49:1–7

Such questions and times of controversy and fatigue are part of the human condition and, upon reflection, probably should not surprise us even with respect to specially chosen servants of God. Such may help us better to understand them and identify with them in our work and ministries. What is perhaps surprising is the way, in practically the same breath, the servant rebounds—sustained by faith that the rightness *(mishpat)* of his cause and recompense is with God. Perhaps it had come to seem that the return from exile would not result in a wonderfully restored Jerusalem of peace and devotion to God. Perhaps the servant felt overwhelmed with the way he was despised and looked down upon by other peoples (see 49:7). Yet, despite appearances, the servant-prophet has faith in God's justice. As we were told in Isa. 42:4, "He will not fail or be discouraged till he has established justice in the earth."

It is typical of the Lord that, instead of offering the servant words of consolation or a lessening of his task in response to his complaint, God ups the challenge. That probably does not seem like good therapy to most schools of psychology, but it may be the best. When people complain about the meager results of their work, give them a greater ministry! "It is too light a thing" (v. 6) that the servant should restore Jacob and bring back the descendants of Israel from the exile. (Isa. 49:7–13 describes this return like a new exodus.) In addition to this national mission there is to be a worldwide ministry. The servant will be made "a light to the nations" (so also in Isa. 42:6 of last week's reading), likely meaning that the vindication of Israel or the servant or both is to be a sign of God's glory (see 49:3) to all the world and to bring them to the worship of the one, true God. That this message is meant for a wide audience is already indicated in the opening verse where it is addressed to the "coastlands" (of Tyre and Phoenicia and perhaps beyond) and "peoples from afar."

In form, Isa. 49:1–6 is reminiscent of other prophetic oracles that begin with a call to hear. It is an announcement that the prophet has a message from God and is the message itself. One senses also the influence of the language of thanksgiving and lament from the Psalms. Not unique in such a pronouncement but still remarkable is the tone of intimacy between the prophet and God, and, despite the momentary lapse into despondency, the confidence the prophet has in God and God's support. God has called him from birth, formed him from the womb, and named him (vv. 1, 5; see Jer. 1:5; Gal. 1:15; Luke 1:15, 31 on God's prenatal call), indicating that the prophet's life and ministry are all part of God's plan. The martial imagery of Isa. 49:2 does not really clash with the humility and tenderness of the servant in Isa. 42:2–3, for these images are meant as analogies. God's purpose is to be established by words and acts of justice. It is less clear why God has hidden the servant—probably to shelter him from enemies.

The riddle of whether the servant is meant to be an individual or corporate figure remains. Some commentators, disturbed by the seeming illogic of the servant being addressed as Israel (v. 3), yet then being given a mission to Israel (v. 5), suggest that the first reference is a later addition. It remains possible, however, that the servant is seen as the corporate body or a remnant of Israel or a representative figure in ways we do not fully comprehend.

Verse 7 begins a new oracle (vv. 7–12) in which it is the Lord who speaks, but the verse fittingly serves as a response to vv. 1–6 in the liturgical lesson. The saving promise of the faithful, Holy One of Israel to one "despaired and abhorred by the nations" links the passage to the song of the suffering servant of Isa. 52:13—53:12, with its picture of the servant "like a lamb (*amnos* in the LXX) that is led to slaughter" (v. 7; see Acts 8:32). For Christians this, in turn, alludes to the "Lamb *(amnos)* of God who takes away the sin of the world" of John 1:29, 36.

GOSPEL: JOHN 1:29–41

If the fourth evangelist has a single reference in mind for John the Baptist's description of Jesus as the Lamb of God, Isa. 53:7 seems the most likely source, but other backgrounds may have played a part, such as the Passover lamb (Exodus 12; see 1 Cor. 5:7), the scapegoat (Lev. 16:21–22, which stands behind Isa. 53:7), and the daily sacrificial lambs of the temple (Exod. 29:38–46; see 1 Pet. 1:19). One also, of course, wonders about a relationship with the lamb of apocalyptic visions in the Revelation of John. In this regard, and in dealing with this passage generally, it is well to remember that the Fourth Gospel is the product of considerable meditation and reflection. It is in some sense the creation of a community of worship that has lived through difficult experiences of persecution and internal controversy. The result is a Gospel with a Christology and other theological perspectives that have emerged from at least two generations of hard Christian living. For them, such images as that of Jesus as the Lamb of God had probably taken on nuances that could no longer be explained by some single background reference. Among its other allusions, the Lamb of God here, at the very beginning of the Gospel, causes hearers to begin to think of saving, sacrificial death to which the Gospel will soon point more specifically.

This period of reflection has also deeply colored the Gospel's presentation of the beginning of Jesus' public ministry. While several features of the story of Jesus' baptism as found in the Synoptic Gospels are present in John the Baptist's confession of Jesus, the baptism itself is not described. Most commentators regard it as presupposed, but why is it not specifically mentioned? In part, this may be the evangelist's way of dealing with the problems Matthew faced in last Sunday's Gospel lesson. Why should the sinless and greater figure (Jesus) be baptized by the lesser (John) for a baptism for the remission of sins? Since this Gospel also has no specific institution of the Lord's Supper, some commentators have also suggested that the evangelist, and perhaps his church, may have been antisacramental. What seems more likely is that the author of the Gospel did not want to suggest that there was a moment or event in historical time in which Jesus became Son of God and received God's favor. Rather, as the Prologue makes clear, he was with God "in the beginning." What John bears witness to is a revelation scene of the one on whom the Holy Spirit descends and remains (*menō,* an important word in this Gospel often translated as "abide" and implying an intimate relationship; see esp. 15:1–10). Jesus not only ranks before John but he "*was* before me." The imperfect tense, which we might try to render as "was being," alludes to the Word's preexistence.

John also has seen and bears witness that Jesus is the Son of God. Jesus' relationship as son to God as father is viewed in this Gospel as signifying a closeness of wills and character—a mutuality and intimacy (see 1:18) that takes on an almost metaphysical character. (It should be noted that a number of manuscripts read "Chosen One of God" instead of "Son of God" in v. 34. This is probably a secondary reading but would link the passage back to the chosen servant of Isa. 42:1).

This Johannine Gospel lesson, which is the exception in the sequence of Matthean readings during the year in the Epiphany season, is intended to help congregations further reflect on the meaning of Jesus' first public manifestation or Epiphany. Preachers might consider these Sundays as an opportunity for a short series of christological sermons on Jesus from both historical and theological perspectives—perhaps bridging into reflections on his basic proclamation and calling of disciples and his ethical teaching in the Sermon on the Mount which follow.

Another of the evangelist's concerns is to establish clearly the relationship between John and Jesus. In addition to his witness to Jesus, John in vv. 19–28 is said to deny that he is the Christ, and, distinct from the Synoptic Gospels, neither is he Elijah, the prophet who was prophesied to come before the day of the Lord (Mal. 4:5). Moreover, we then hear (vv. 35–41) that the first two of Jesus' disciples had been disciples of John. Scholars have long been intrigued by this information. It suggests a more intricate relationship between what we might call the Jesus movement and the Baptist movement than the Synoptic Gospels indicate. While, on the one hand, scholars suspect that this evangelist may have some useful historical insights in this regard, and his tradition may have had some association with an ongoing Baptist movement, on the other hand—and just for these reasons—this Gospel may well be seeking to clarify the relationship from a theological perspective which simplifies the historical complexities.

Preachers could use the occasion to reflect with their congregations on the ministry of the Baptist (who is, in fact, not given this title in the Fourth Gospel), perhaps thinking of what it means to make clear who one is not in order to witness to who Jesus is. However complex the historical relationship between John and Jesus and their groups of followers may have been, it would seem that John did at some point exalt the role of Jesus. The ministry of witnessing *(martyria)* plays a consistent role from the beginning to the end of this Gospel, and the preacher might also think about the historical and contemporary aspects of being a witness by word and deed. The word *(martyria, martyreō)* is critical to John the Baptist's ministry in this chapter (vv. 7, 8, 15, 19, 33, 34) and certainly belongs to the Epiphany season's emphasis on the showing forth and manifestation of who Jesus was and is. The true witness does not just observe but finds ways to make known the importance and significance of what is seen. Witnessing is an active role, and in the developing life of the churches to be a witness came to mean witnessing even unto death, and so our word *martyr.* Certainly not every Christian will be called to give such a witness, but a helpful sermon would describe various kinds of witnessing in a variety of circumstances in today's world.

John's witness also brings Jesus' first disciples to him, and the willingness of Andrew to tell his brother about Jesus begins to expand the circle of discipleship. Several of the lectionaries lengthen the reading on to John 1:41, and one could reflect on what it means to become a disciple. Jesus' words to them, "Come and see" (repeated by Philip in v. 46), are particularly pregnant, suggesting the importance of a personal following. One also notices how the disciples' understanding progresses in these verses from seeing Jesus as a great teacher to knowing him to be the Messiah. This adds to the christological dimensions of the entire lection.

EPISTLE: 1 CORINTHIANS 1:1–9

The opening portion of Paul's First Letter to the Corinthians also tells about the meaning of discipleship in exalted tones of thanksgiving for God's gifts. The passage contains as well the word *martyria* ("witness" or "testimony"), enabling a good association with that theme in the other readings. Members of the church in Corinth are "sanctified in Christ Jesus and called to be saints" (v. 2). Who they are is the result of God's "grace . . . given in (or "by" or "through") Christ," enriching them "with all speech and all knowledge . . . so that you are not lacking in any spiritual gift" (vv. 4, 5, 7). The calling to be holy is God's initiative. It comes to every member of the church and *calls* them also (v. 9) into a community *(koinōnia)* of personal relationship with God's Son, Jesus Christ our Lord. Paul stresses that God is "faithful" in this calling and that Jesus will sustain the disciples to the end, "guiltless (or "blameless" or "irreproachable"; see Col. 1:22 and, with respect to deacons, elders, and bishops, 1 Tim. 3:10; Titus 1:6, 7) in the day of our Lord Jesus Christ" (vv. 8–9). Together with the word "revealing" *(apokalypsis* in v. 7) one notes the strong eschatological tone here, a reminder to the Corinthians not only of how God strengthens and preserves them, but of the final time of judgment—the end time.

One could also at this time focus attention on the sanctified, "called to be saints," and *koinōnia* character of the whole church of God and of the particular representation of it in each place. What does it mean to be such a church as part of the whole *koinōnia* in today's world? A sermon might take the form of a letter in which the preacher thinks of himself or herself as absent for a time and writes from a distance to remind the congregation of who they are called to be.

Those with knowledge of the entire Corinthian correspondence cannot, however, hear these words without a sense of irony. While God's saving action makes the Corinthians sanctified ones, they are far from perfect in human perspective. In his prayer of thanksgiving (vv. 4–9), which follows the greeting of vv. 1–3, Paul introduces themes that will have a more controversial character in the subsequent correspondence. Questions of whose speech is truly powerful (Paul's or the "superlative apostles") and about the relationship between edifying speech and tongues, about women speaking in church, and the purpose and character of spiritual gifts are all on the agenda (2 Cor. 10:10—11:6; 1 Cor. 11:2—14:39). The meaning of genuine knowledge *(gnōsis)* is later contrasted with a knowledge that "puffs up" (see 1 Cor. 8:1–11; 12:8; 13:2, 8; 14:6). In the next verses (1 Cor. 1:10–17) we find that the *koinōnia* of this church is marred by divisions.

The fact of the matter is that the Corinthians have fallen into several of the traps that await "the saints," especially in thinking of themselves as having more knowledge and being more skilled in spiritual matters than others. In one sense, as Paul's introductory prayer of thanksgiving effusively says, this is true. God is gracious and generous to those whom God calls. Yet, on the other hand, all this *giftedness* is from God. Christians may have different manifestations of the Spirit, but it is "the same Spirit" and all disciples are essentially equal and parts of the one body of Christ. All gifts must be infused with the highest gift of love. (See 1 Cor. 12:4—13:13.) Even the word "enriched" in 1 Cor. 1:5 takes on ironic overtones when it later seems evident that some of the Corinthians are saying things such as, "We are filled! We are rich! We have become kings!" (1 Cor. 4:8) and using their sense of exalted status to distinguish themselves as superior to inferior Christians.

We will have more to say about this fascinating Corinthian church as we proceed. Passages from the first four chapters of First Corinthians offer lections for the next six Sundays of Epiphany, and the preacher may want to remember that subsequent chapters from this letter are the source of Epiphany readings in years B and C. Part of the Corinthians' interest for us lies in the fact that we have more correspondence to them than to any other church. We know yet more about their city from other sources and from considerable recent sociological analysis. In many ways, too, their problems over questions of immorality, divisions, mores, spiritual gifts, and so on, at least parallel scandals, problems, and struggles in church life today. Nor did the problems end with Paul's correspondence. Writing a little more than a generation later, Clement of Rome indicates that the Corinthians persisted in being a fractious and contentious bunch (see 1 Clem. 1:1; 3; 46:9; 47:5–7). In new forms the issues have persisted and continue in our own churches. Perhaps the preacher might want to make some of them part of the letter-sermon suggested earlier. When telling of the meaning of witnessing and showing forth the Lord in the Epiphany season, problems and difficulties cannot be left out of the whole picture.

The Third Sunday after the Epiphany

Lutheran	Roman Catholic	Episcopal	Common Lectionary
Isa. 9:1b–4	Isa. 8:23b—9:3	Amos 3:1–8	Isa. 9:1–4
1 Cor. 1:10–17	1 Cor. 1:10–13, 17	1 Cor. 1:10–17	1 Cor. 1:10–17
Matt. 4:12–23	Matt. 4:12–23	Matt. 4:12–23	Matt. 4:12–23

What gives people hope? Many regions of the world have known the deep gloom that Galilee experienced. Yet it does not require a massive amount of radiance to make a light that can transform the darkness. A few rays of sun breaking through heavy clouds to shine upon a small field can make all the difference.

A number of people have had the experience of being out on a pitch–dark night. They are in an unfamiliar countryside trying to find their way to a friend's house, where they have never been before. They feel lost; the darkness around them is a vast void. The road seems endless. They are afraid of falling off into a ditch. At last they see in the distance a point of light. It comes from the window of a house. They are no longer alone, and suddenly all the darkness about them is changed. It is no longer everything, but what they pass through on the way to the light.

FIRST LESSON: ISAIAH 9:1–4

Today's reading from the Jewish Scriptures has been chosen to fit the Matthean lesson, which somewhat loosely quotes several of its lines. After the prose introduction of Isa. 9:1, which sets the locale, vv. 2–7 are a prophetic oracle especially familiar because of the last two verses telling of the birth of the ideal king. Our truncated portion of the prophecy offers but the first of three reasons for new hope and celebration: the yoke and collar of servitude and the driver's rod or goad have been broken (v. 4). Together with the destruction of battle gear (v. 5) and the birth of the crown prince (vv. 6–7), this tells why a great light now is shining upon the area of the northern tribes.

The vision in several ways transcends historical time. The perfect tenses are "prophetic perfects," which tell of something that so certainly will come to pass that it is already present. The time is after the Assyrian King Tiglath-pileser III had conquered and annexed the northern area of the old Israelite kingdom. This area was generally referred to as the *galil* (so 2 Kings 15:29), the "circle" or "district," later as Galilee. It was already called "Galilee of the nations" because so many foreigners lived there.

The "way of the seal" refers to the road, used by conquering armies, that led from Syria to the Mediterranean.

Isaiah may have been an official priest-prophet of the Jerusalem court. In any case he was an advisor of kings and here prophesies of a new day in which people will rejoice as at harvest time or when soldiers divide the spoil. The end of the oppression is likened to Gideon's victory over the Midianites described in Judg. 7:16–25.

GOSPEL: MATTHEW 4:12–23

By Jesus' and Matthew's time "Galilee of the nations" was an even more apt description because the area had been ruled after the Assyrians by the Babylonians, Persians, Macedonians, and by Egypt and Syria. Although for a time the Hasmoneans had put much of the area under control from Jerusalem, and there had been something of a Jewish repopulation, the region had finally come under Roman dominance, governed by client kings and later procurators, and was known for its heterogeneous population.

Although there are more than a few signs in Matthew's Gospel that the early Christian message was seen as exclusively for Jews, and some of the tension from that understanding continued into Matthew's time, the evangelist himself seems to have had a worldwide mission firmly in view. This is clarion clear at the conclusion of his Gospel ("Go therefore and make disciples of all nations"; 28:19), and Matthew signals the same message as Jesus begins his ministry. Jesus' home region is thus seen as symbolic for the wider mission to all peoples. This symbolism, of course, fits well into the overall theme of the Epiphany season of showing forth Christ to the world.

It seems credible that the end of John the Baptist's ministry may have in some way prompted Jesus to a more public role or given him more prominence. He centers his ministry on his home area but leaves the hill country for the more populous cities and towns about Lake Galilee. There is indication in all the Gospels that Capernaum now virtually became his hometown.

With his frequently used Scripture citation formula ". . . that what was spoken by the prophet———might be fulfilled," Matthew quotes Isa. 9:1–2. It is thought that Matthew may have had a compilation of such fulfillment texts which he incorporated into his Gospel. His point is not so much that Jesus fulfills scriptural promise as that the promise is fulfilled in him. Matthew wishes to show that what happened was all part of God's plan of salvation.

The evangelist now summarizes Jesus' mission: (1) He proclaims the basic message, evidently taken over from the Baptist (see Matt. 3:2),

"Repent, for the kingdom of heaven is at hand." (2) He calls disciples. (3) Jesus travels about, and, along with preaching the *evangelion* ("good news") of the kingdom, he teaches and heals. Much of what Matthew records in the rest of his Gospel will show Jesus doing this teaching and healing. In particular, the subsequent "Sermon on the Mount" (chaps. 5— 7) is a compendium of his ethical instruction, followed in chap. 8 by the healing of a Jewish leper, the servant of a Gentile centurion, and then Peter's mother-in-law. Together these words and acts help hearers to understand why Jesus "taught them with authority, and not as their scribes" (Matt. 7:29).

This same ministry of preaching the kingdom and healing is given to the disciples (Matt. 10:1–15) and, along with the calling of disciples, serves as a useful summary for the mission of the church, past and present. The kingdom of God (Matthew regularly uses "of heaven" [literally "heavens"], a Jewish way of avoiding God's name which may reflect Jesus' own language) is not a place or an abstract idea, but rather "the ruling of God," God's activity and purpose in the world. In an important sense God is not known directly in Jesus' teaching, but the activity of God—God's righteousness, forgiveness, and concern for true justice—reveals the character of God.

This understanding of God's reign was not new. What still seems startling, however, is Jesus' passionate (almost breathless in his words) conviction that this reign "is at hand." The Greek verb *engiken* is in the perfect tense. In a sense it is another "prophetic perfect" and indicates the result of something that has already happened or begun to happen. "The reign of God has drawn near."

One looks for analogies. It is as if Christmas is at hand. It is not December 25 yet, but the fact that it is only ten days (seven shopping days!) away has begun dramatically to affect our lives and plans. I tell my students that the examination has been moved up to next Tuesday. It hasn't happened yet, but suddenly the way they look at the coming weekend is radically altered. Joy and testing are at hand.

Doubtless, for many people the kingdom seemed an impossible dream. At best, God's justice and peace would be known on some future great day or they exist only beyond this life "in the heavens." Jesus' proclamation wound the clock so tightly that the kingdom became so near it had already begun. God's ruling was breaking into this time and place. It was not just a goal, but what was happening. The new time was now. Righteousness and fairness were not just what might await one at the end of life, but the ways in which life was to be lived now. They were the means to the end.

Still, people did not believe. In the face of so much evil and injustice, how could God's ruling be at hand? People, Jesus contended, needed new ways of hearing and seeing. He told parables about the kingdom and did healings as symbolic acts showing that the promised time of God was begun. The kingdom's ways were often different from what many expected. What surprised and even angered a number of Jesus' contemporaries was the way the kingdom's advent upset many human judgments about what was fair and right, especially with regard to who was included in the kingdom's offer. Jesus seemed to want to include everyone—the physically disabled (whose condition some regarded as a sign of God's disfavor) and people of questionable professions and life-styles. Those who wanted to put themselves first by excluding others would find they had so excluded themselves.

Jesus' passionate concern seems to have been to restore and prepare the whole people of Israel for what God was now doing. Repentance was at once a condition of preparation and what was enabled by the good news that the kingdom was at hand. The English word "repentance" does not catch all the nuances of the Greek word *(metanoia),* which signified change of mind, a change in the way of viewing life. Nor does "repentance" quite translate the Aramaic and Hebrew words that picture a turning to a new direction. The New Testament understanding of "repentance" affects the manner in which one views past actions, but it is more concerned with present and future attitudes. One has a new way of thinking and hoping and living because God's reign has drawn near. This new hope and life is open to all—no matter what their past is like. Not only in word but in his actions Jesus extended that offer to the blind, lame, demon-possessed, prostitutes, tax gatherers, and others. He offered it to them so they could "repent," gaining new hope and changed lives. For this he earned the surprise and often the ire of religious contemporaries who held that such people could not be included in the true community of the people of God until they had demonstrated changed lives. If the old religious message went something like, Be good, and then God will accept you, the ministry of Jesus said, God accepts you into new relationship in the kingdom at hand; now be good. Now you can be good.

But there is not much time to make this choice. The urgency in Jesus' words and actions comes from his conviction that God's ways and the demands of the kingdom are now a part of human life. Although Matthew's perspective and later church experience lengthened the time frame in one sense, the imperative remains that NOW is the only time one lives and can decide.

The urgency is underscored by the manner in which two sets of brothers immediately leave their nets and follow Jesus, becoming his first disciples. One may imagine that the actual life situation was a bit more complex— the decision to go with Jesus not quite so instantaneous. Yet the story may well leave the correct overall impression. Response to his urgent message and his person was swift and life changing. One also notices that the words "Follow me" (Matt. 4:19) are here and in John 21:19, 22 the first and last words Jesus speaks to his disciples.

Preachers will ask how this message of the kingdom can best be heard and enacted in today's churches. What healings of physical and mental illnesses and the problems that cause them are now to be practiced as part of the proclamation and teaching of the Gospel? After Jesus' death and resurrection, after his followers have come to see that he not only told of the kingdom but in many ways personally revealed the character of God's reign, and after the possibilities of the kingdom's nearing in the message of and about Jesus have been opened to all people, what is to be the nature of Christian community?

EPISTLE: 1 CORINTHIANS 1:10–17

Certainly it does not help in the offering of that message when Christians are seen to be squabbling and lacking in agreement. One does not know which is worse—serious theological disagreement or bickering about personality, money, and territory. Church history teaches us that sometimes the theological differences seem to follow the more personal disagreements and are used to justify divisions based on language, culture, or economics. What was taking place in Corinth appears to be based more in personalities—perhaps in class and background. We can do little more than guess, but the present-day analogies with our guesses may be instructive.

Some say, "I belong to Paul." Some put loyalty to the founding personality above all else. This is certainly understandable. In how many churches today is the congregation built around the personality of the founding or long-time pastor? Loyalty to that figure becomes a test of loyalty to the church. Many people want a father or mother figure. Few pastors escape feeling the tug of that role. While television evangelists are not physically present for this role, it is even easier for some people to almost worship them. Their weaknesses and faults cannot (unless suddenly exposed!) be seen on television.

Paul does not entirely escape the subtle pulls of the role, but he sees its dangers. It can lead disciples to concentrate on the wrong figure (Was Paul crucified for you?) and the wrong issues. Unavoidably, some will feel closer to Paul than others and so put others in a secondary role. In another letter to the Corinthians Paul sets the issue in this perspective: "For what we preach is not ourselves, but Jesus Christ as Lord, with ourselves as your servants for Jesus' sake. . . . We have this treasure in earthen vessels, to show that the transcendent power belongs to God and not to us" (2 Cor. 4:5, 7).

Some say, "I belong to Apollos." In addition to having been in Corinth more recently, Apollos, one can imagine, might have appealed to the more intellectual group of Corinthians. Paul evidently was accused by some of having preached too simple a gospel message (1 Cor. 3:1–2). We are told in Acts 18:24–28 of Apollos's eloquence and knowledge of the Scriptures. Coming from Alexandria, where Philo had only recently died, Apollos was perhaps an expert in allegorical interpretation. Although fervent in his preaching, he evidently did not know about baptism in the Holy Spirit, and it may be that the more charismatically inclined Corinthians felt that they were closer to Paul or to another group.

Others say, "I belong to Cephas." This group may have been more conservative. They may have been the more Jewish element in the community, feeling closer to the Jerusalem church. Although there is no other indication that Peter himself had come to Corinth, his name may be connected with those whom Paul archly calls "these superlative apostles" (2 Cor. 11:5; 12:11), who were probably Jewish-Christians from Jerusalem and claimed a more powerful, authentic gospel message.

Still others say, "I belong to Christ." Paul may have been making a tongue-in-cheek suggestion when he said that some claimed they belong to Christ alone. But why, one wonders, didn't Paul advise them all to say that they belonged to Christ? What may well have been happening is that some were setting themselves up as the true believers in the church whose dedication to Christ exceeded that of all others.

These divisions manifested themselves in other ways in Corinth. There were the weak of conscience and the strong with regard to eating meat that had been offered to idols (1 Corinthians 8—10). There were differences about speaking in tongues, spiritual gifts generally (1 Corinthians 12—14), and other matters. Paul does not want the Corinthians to get bogged down in jealousy, strife, and personality issues. The Corinthians are behaving in all too human a way when one says, "I belong to Paul," and another, "I belong to Apollos" (1 Cor. 3:3–4). "What then is Apollos? What is Paul? Servants through whom you believed. . . . For we are God's fellow workers; you are God's field, God's building. . . . For no other foundation can anyone lay than . . . Christ Jesus" (1 Cor. 3:5, 9, 11).

In other images, especially that of the body of Christ (Rom. 12:4–8; 1 Cor. 12:4–31), Paul presents his understanding of the essential unity of all Christians. With a diversity of gifts each has their role to play. None should be "puffed up in favor of one against another" for all gifts are from God (1 Cor. 4:6–7). All members are parts of the one body, and gifts are to be used for the edification of the church (see also Eph. 4:15–16). Paul rightly recognizes how some link their party membership to their baptism and so later reminds the Corinthians that "by one Spirit we were all baptized into one body . . . and all were made to drink of one Spirit" (1 Cor. 12:13; see Eph. 4:4–6).

It is fortuitous that 1 Cor. 1:10–17 is read during the Week of Prayer for Christian Unity. It is a useful opportunity to reflect on the causes of disunity and the opportunities for mission in faith and action through Christian unity.

The Fourth Sunday after the Epiphany

Lutheran	Roman Catholic	Episcopal	Common Lectionary
Mic. 6:1–8	Zeph. 2:3; 3:12–13	Mic. 6:1–8	Mic. 6:1–8
1 Cor. 1:26–31	1 Cor. 1:26–31	1 Cor. 1:26–31	1 Cor. 1:18–31
Matt. 5:1–12	Matt. 5:1–12a	Matt. 5:1–12	Matt. 5:1–12

Who are the humble poor of this world? Why are they blessed? Are disciples meant to join with them, become them, help them? These are questions that any thoughful hearer of today's lessons will have in mind. They are critical questions for the life of the church. They speak directly to vital issues: how people are to live and serve the purposes of God.

ALTERNATIVE FIRST LESSON: ZEPHANIAH 2:3; 3:12–13

Zephaniah was perhaps the most doom-and-gloom prophet of Judah. Some scholars wonder whether the verses that offer a glimmer of hope were not added by later hands. Probably active in the first part of Josiah's reign (perhaps in the decade 631–621), Zephaniah condemned the ruling groups (court officials, royal figures, merchants, judges, prophets, and priests) in Judah who permitted and pursued corrupt religious practices. Also condemned are the nations for their pride and insults to God's people. Only the humble *(anawim)* of the land, who do God's commands, and seek righteousness and humility, may be hidden or sheltered on the "day" (a quasitechnical prophetic term for the time of judgment) of the Lord's anger (2:3).

In the third chapter that surviving remnant is further described (vv. 11–13). These people, humbled and poor *(ani)* because of their affliction, will not be put to shame on account of the proud and haughty. The humble poor will be rid of them. Those who take refuge in the Lord will not be engaged in wrongdoing, lies, or deceit. In a familiar biblical image, they shall have pasture to feed in and find rest and security (see Isa. 40:11; Ezek. 34:11–16; Zech. 11:7). The Lord thus rejects the proud and corrupt, but the poor and those who do God's commands, seeking righteousness and true humility, will be the survivors.

FIRST LESSON: MICAH 6:1–8

In a different tone and context, Mic. 6:1–8 offers a similar lesson. Verses 1–5 are like the beginning of a lawsuit. In vv. 1–2 the prophet calls the people to hear of the Lord's controversy with them. In vv. 3–5 the Lord reminds the people of the saving acts that have been done for them. Clearly, they have forgotten what the Lord has accomplished for the people and what their response should be. In vv. 6–7 a worshiper asks what the Lord wants. With what offerings and sacrifices should the worshiper approach the Lord? "God has shown you what is good *(tov)*" and what is required. The implication is that what now follows is a summary of the essence of the Torah and all God's dealings with Israel: "To do justice *(mishpat)*, to love kindness. . . ."*Hesed*, often translated as "lovingkindness," is learned from the favor God has shown. The word also connotes mercy and suggests a loyalty of relationship. In a sense *mishpat* is doing all the law requires, and the love (not just observance) of *hesed* implies going further to a still more personal caring and relationship. "To walk humbly with your God" is in a sense another description of doing justice and lovingkindness. It means to walk thoughtfully (not stooped over; see v. 6) in the doing of God's will of justice and lovingkindness. It means to be properly dependent on God in one's life and actions.

GOSPEL: MATTHEW 5:1–12

Both the Zephaniah and Micah readings are clearly intended to point toward and help in the understanding of the Beatitudes. These blessings stand at the head of Matthew's famous Sermon on the Mount (chaps. 5—7). This sermon is the first of five major teaching sections in Matthew's Gospel, all clearly marked off by the concluding words ". . . when Jesus finished these sayings." Understandably, it has been thought that Matthew is in this manner suggesting that Jesus is like a new Moses with his five teachings comparable to the five books of the Pentateuch. Matthew was probably not thinking of these as a new law but as the new and right interpretation of the spirit and meaning of the law by Jesus.

The sermon is most likely a compilation from several sources and traditions brought together by Matthew to help his hearers understand Jesus' emphases and interpretations. It is mainly ethical teaching, but one also finds a prayer and counsel in the forms of wisdom sayings and parabolic analogy.

It is important to try to understand who is being addressed by the Sermon and the Beatitudes in particular. In the most significant sense it is, of course, Matthew's audience—presumably his church of Jewish and Gentile Christians seeking to interpret their lives and calling some two generations after the resurrection. Within the Gospel it is not wholly clear whether Matthew has in mind the crowds following Jesus (4:25—5:1) or the disciples who came to him on the mountain. The latter group (in this sense already committed followers) is probably meant to be the primary audience with perhaps the understanding that the crowds (the larger society) can at least listen.

The question of audience becomes still more significant when one recalls the Lukan form of four blessings (Luke 6:20–23). They are addressed directly to the disciples using the second-person plural, "Blessed are you. . . ." Matthew's version allows the understanding that it might be the poor and meek of the larger world who are being called blessed. Luke seems to confine this blessedness to the group of disciples.

What the Beatitudes so clearly set forth is a startling reversal of human ways of valuing. Some forms of religion have regularly suggested that the goods and honors of this world are signs of divine favor. Here the exclamations regarding who is blessed fall in the first three or four Beatitudes on the have-nots. Statements of blessedness are fairly frequent in the Jewish Scriptures (see, e.g., Pss. 1:1; 2:12; 84:4; 119:2; Prov. 8:32). There, and for the most part in Matthew as well, the word does not so much convey a blessing as to state the circumstances of the group or individual and, probably, God's attitude toward them.

Matthew is sometimes thought to have spiritualized his understanding of who the poor are by the addition of the words "in spirit" (not found in Luke 6:20). This addition could mean one of several things: those who are, as it were, broken in spirit, or those who know their need of God, or perhaps it may be meant to be inclusive of even wealthy people if they have the right spiritual attitude toward the goods of this world. It is more likely that the two words are intended to help hearers understand "poor" in the sense in which we have found it used in Zephaniah. It refers to those who are powerless and who are afflicted by the wealthy and strong in society. They almost surely will be poor in goods, too, but the emphasis falls on their marginality. The understanding of their status is further interpreted by "those who mourn" in the next beatitude and by "the meek." The importance of humility or a kind of gentleness is stressed in Mic. 6:8 and also Isa. 66:2. It connotes a proper dependence on God. In the Zephaniah reading such humbleness accompanies the condition of being poor

in those whom God will help survive and who will find pasture. In the
first three Beatitudes even more is involved. These blessed ones have the
promised kingdom; they shall be comforted and have the earth for their
possession. It is difficult to say exactly what this means for them, but it
is, above all, a sign of God's favor and the promise of God's care.

What does this reversal of values tell disciples hearing this message?
Are only those in this condition blessed? Should others then, who may not
be marginalized or mourning, try to join them? In what ways? Or are those
who seem more fortunate in their participation in the wealth of the world
to recognize God's special care and favor for the poor and humble and so
seek to side with them in life's struggles? Again, in what ways? One
realizes how much we have learned from the liberation theologians. The
contemporary context in which the passage is heard is critical. It cannot
fail to be heard differently in a well-to-do suburban church from the way
a house church in a poverty-stricken barrio will hear it. Perhaps what the
passage should most help the suburban congregation understand is that
they ought to try also to hear it as it is heard by their brothers and sisters
in the barrio or slum.

The next beatitude (v. 6) probably refers to the have-nots as well. Luke
(6:21) speaks of the physically hungry, but Matthew may well intend those
who experience no righteousness and justice in their lives. It is also possible
to understand the pronouncement in a more active sense and so to link it
with the next four beatitudes. Those who seek the righteousness *(dikaiosynē)*
of God, for themselves and others, shall be fulfilled. The word *dikaiosynē*
resounds with the other uses Matthew gives it in these beatitudes (v. 10),
elsewhere in the sermon (5:20; 6:1, 33), and in his Gospel (3:15; 21:32).
one thinks, too, of Paul's frequent use of the word as God's "righteousness"
and as "being made right" with God. (See 1 Cor. 1:30 in today's second
reading, and also recall the *sedakah* [righteousness] of Zeph. 2:3.)

Being peacemakers (esp. here as reconcilers in strife situations) and
showing mercy are themes more easily understood by direct translation to
our lives. Being merciful is based on the experience of God's mercy and
causes one to think of the mutuality of forgiveness in the petition of the
Lord's Prayer (Matt. 6:12). Matthew twice has Jesus quote Hos. 6:6, "I
desire mercy and not sacrifice."

"Pure in heart" suggests a singleness of will and purpose with respect
to God's will. Certainly for Matthew (see 15:16–20 and again the quotations
of Hos. 6:6), and often in Judaism, it is not an outward ritual purity that
counts with God (see, e.g., Ps. 24:3–4).

The final beatitude (v. 10) is expounded in vv. 11–12 in the second-
person plural, here clearly meant to include the experience of the disciples.

They are linked to the poor of v. 3 since theirs, too, is the kingdom of heaven.

Every Christian individual and community is bound to be tested by hearing the Beatitudes. Several of them may seem quite acceptable, if not easy to adopt as standards for one's life. Others more severely challenge values regarding what is worthy, strong, and commendable in a culture now often only vaguely familiar with Christian teachings. Again, many North American hearers will have to recognize that they need the help of the poor and meek and mourning in today's world to help them understand and act on the Beatitudes. All Christians also recognize that a good part of the power of the Beatitudes comes from the awareness that Jesus is believed not only to have spoken them but to have lived them.

EPISTLE: 1 CORINTHIANS 1:18–31

Paul also has some helpful thoughts to share on what it means to be humble, dependent on God, and to recognize one's essential poverty, but his words are directed in a somewhat polemical manner to a particular group of Christians. Some of the Corinthians, he fears, have forgotten how they were called to redemption.

The Common Lectionary includes vv. 18–25 and makes the direct connection with last Sunday's reading. Paul had heard about the quarreling and divisions in Corinth. In vv. 18–31 they are still very much on his mind. A major cause of the dissensions was evidently the belief of some of the Corinthians that they had gained a stature and wisdom that set them apart from and made them superior to others. They may have felt they had leaders who were highly articulate with respect to this wisdom. We recall, too, that groups of the Corinthians were apparently identifying themselves on the basis of who baptized them. Thus in v. 17 Paul maintains that his primary ministry is not to baptize "but to preach the gospel, and not with eloquent wisdom, lest the cross of Christ be emptied of its power."

The mention of "wisdom" and "power" causes him to reflect on what is true power and wisdom by Christian standards and what is false. The wisdom of the world would ask for something very different from the crucified Christ. It would want a more universal and abstract way of talking about God's presence in human life. Nor would such a Christ be one expected by those who look for signs and power in the world's terms. Thus, to the Jews demanding signs, Christ crucified is a stumbling block, while to Greeks seeking wisdom he is folly. Yet Christ is the power and wisdom of God.

In this contrast of worldly values and those revealed in Christ one feels close to the tenor of the Beatitudes and the words of Zephaniah. God's grace is known to the humble poor. Paul now reminds the Corinthians that this is what they were and remain.

We do not know the specific circumstances of the Corinthian converts. They evidently were not all slaves or destitute. Paul stayed with Aquila and Priscilla, and they together practiced the rather middle-class trade of tentmaking. Titius Justus had a house. Crispus was the ruler of the synagogue (see Acts 18:1–8). Chloe may have headed a considerable household, and there was also the household of Stephanas (1 Cor. 1:11, 16). Nevertheless, the bulk of the membership probably did come from the lower economic and social classes. Not many would have had much education. Paul wants them to remember this and, whatever their class, to realize that it was not because of education or birth or money that God chose them. Indeed, God's power is best shown by choosing what seems weak, foolish, and ignoble in the world. One thinks of Paul's words later in this correspondence: "We have this treasure in earthen vessels to show that the transcendent power belongs to God and not to us" (2 Cor. 4:7). Through an experience of physical debility, the Lord teaches Paul that "my power is made perfect in weakness" (2 Cor. 12:9).

In rhetorical tones, Paul insists that God chooses what is "lowborn and contemptible in the world, mere nothings" (v. 29). It is not clear that he is still talking specifically about the Corinthians, but they could not help but feel the allusions. One has to contrast what Paul had to say in the introduction of this letter (for us but two Sundays ago) about the calling of the Corinthians to be saints and the manner in which they were enriched with all speech and all knowledge. But what Paul is now practically rubbing their noses in is the awareness that their gifts are not their own—not what they are to boast of. Therefore, "Let the one who boasts, boast of the Lord" (v. 31, quoting Jer. 9:23–24). It is Jesus Christ, the one who was crucified, whom God has made "our wisdom, our righteousness (see Matt. 5:6, 10; Zeph. 2:3) and sanctification (*hagiasmos,* i.e., "saint making") and redemption" (see Rom. 3:24; 8:23). So do the poor of this world discover that theirs is the kingdom of God.

The author of the fourteenth-century mystical treatise *The Cloud of Unknowing* held that "Only to our intellect is God incomprehensible, not to our love" (chap. 4). Thomas Aquinas tried to explain this mystery by contrasting the action of the intellect as a movement that takes into itself in order to comprehend. It thus reduces what it thinks of to the intellect's own limitations. Love, on the other hand, must move out beyond itself and so begins to discover that which is greater than the self, that which transcends the self (see *Summa Theologics,* I.I.20 art. 2 and II.II.66 art 6). So may disciples begin to have some awareness of why the gift of relationship must come from God and be known by love rather than human wisdom.

The Fifth Sunday after the Epiphany

Lutheran	Roman Catholic	Episcopal	Common Lectionary
Isa. 58:5–9a	Isa. 58:7–10	Hab. 3:1–6, 17-19	Isa. 58:3–9a
1 Cor. 2:1–5	1 Cor. 2:1–5	1 Cor. 2:1–11	1 Cor. 2:1–11
Matt. 5:13–20	Matt. 5:13–16	Matt. 5:13–20	Matt. 5:13–16

These are dangerous lessons! Each in its own way raises critical questions about the forms and practice of religion in relation to the will of God. The lessons are dangerous because they will be read and commented upon in modern-day situations where it remains all too easy for both the preachers and congregations to "be religious"—to have all the words and ceremony—without much true religion. How does the community let the true light of God show in the world? In the Epiphany season it is especially appropriate to ask how a people can become the light of and for the world by reflecting the glory of God. But how is that done without just the appearance of advertising and self-glorification?

Hearing Isaiah's words, one may well recall the admonition from the Johannine disciple: "If anyone says, 'I love God' and hates their brother or sister, that person is a liar; for those who do not love their own brother or sister whom they have seen, cannot love God whom they have not seen" (1 John 4:20). One might also remember James's critique of those who claim to have faith though without works to show for it. "If a brother or sister is ill-clad and in lack of daily food, and one of you says to them, 'Go in peace, be warmed and filled,' without giving them the things needed for the body, what does it profit?" (James 2:15–16). Jesus powerfully illustrates the same concern in his parable about the segregation of those who gave food and drink to the hungry and thirsty, welcomed them when welcoming strangers, clothed the naked, visited the sick and prisoners, from those who did not do these things (Matt. 25:31–46). With such teaching the New Testament is setting forth again the repeated demand of the prophets for what God requires. Fasts, sacrifices, feast days, solemn assemblies are only acceptable to God when justice and mercy are being done (see Isa. 1:10–17; Jer. 7:16–26; Psalm 50; Amos 5:21–24; Mic. 6:6–8; Zech. 7:1–14).

FIRST LESSON: ISAIAH 58:5–10

What could be more religious than a fast? It demands sacrifice and discipline. It is done in the Lord's name. Although the Pentateuch seems to know of only one fast, that of the Day of Atonement (Lev. 23:26–32; Num. 29:7), fasting on important occasions (before battles, in times of drought or other threats, at dedications) was a well-known practice, both in Israel and in other nations. (In addition to the passages referred to above, see Judg. 20:26; 2 Sam. 12:16, 22; Jon. 3:6–10; Joel 2:12–14; Neh. 9:1.)

In a rather primitive way, a fast may be undertaken to attract God's attention and try to get God to do something rather than being undertaken to help people become better attuned to God's will. Isaiah 58:3 is probably critical of such a practice put so crudely in the mouth of the people. Then comes the next criticism: The people are not doing anything to change their ways during their fasting. They are pursuing their commercial interests by means involving oppression of workers (v. 3).

Fighting and bickering go on apace—perhaps abetted by the crabbiness people can feel when fasting (v. 4). Verse 5 may even seem to question the very idea of fasting, certainly if it is a substitute for fairness and sharing. The Hebrew plays on the similar sound of the words *ṣom* (fast) and *yom* (day) with all the overtones of this latter word as the day of the Lord's judgment (see Amos 5:18). What is the value of all this bowing down and apparent humbling of the self (v. 5)?

It is interesting that there is no mention of the temple, sacrifices, or other cultic activities in this passage. (The right observance of the sabbath is discussed in vv. 13–15.) Likely, this is because the temple has not yet been rebuilt. The time is still shortly after the end of the exile. The circumstances of life may well have been a disappointment for anyone who thought a golden age was just around the corner following the exile. (That is why they are fasting: to get God to make things better!) These conditions probably made it all the more difficult to hear the prophet's call for those who had managed to secure some of life's necessities and a slight hold on security. But in these circumstances those with some possessions had a number of kin (perhaps some of them recently returned from exile) without sufficient food, housing, or clothing. To leave them in such a state meant not only that they were destitute, but that they were the easy victims of oppression and a virtual slavery. They had no means to help themselves.

The prophet points out that those who are suffering are "your own flesh" from whom their kin ought not hide themselves. The language prompts the imagination to think of the ways one hides from the poverty of others today, and the preacher might want to reflect on our contemporary ways of doing so: by living in especially zoned residential areas away from poverty; by means of economic theories suggesting that only an "invisible hand" or market forces can enable the poor to help themselves, perhaps with the implication that it is their fault for the circumstances they are in; by denying that we are one flesh. It is a favorite human strategy when denying aid to others to contend that they are not of our clan or race or religion or citizenship. Presumably it would have been difficult for the people of Jerusalem and its neighborhood to do this, but still they may have—perhaps by treating some of those come back from exile as not fully of their group. Or maybe it was the other way around, with those who had returned wanting to hide from the poverty of those who had inhabited the Jerusalem area during the exile.

Some ethicists may worry about the manner in which sharing with the needy is said to be rewarded by the Lord in this passage. Should not showing mercy and doing justice be their own reward? In an important sense, however, that is what the passage intends. By caring for all its members the people will become the kind of community God wishes them to be. This will make them strong and help them to rebuild in both spiritual and physical ways. They will know the Lord's presence (v. 9) and their light will break forth and be seen. Here as elsewhere (see 52:12 with respect to the Lord going before and being a rear guard in v. 8) this prophetic voice echoes the hopes of the author of Isaiah 40—55. Those dreams will come true when the people are a people of charity and justice. Then they may be a "light to the nations" (Isa. 42:6; 49:6). They will shine with the Lord's glory by reflecting God's character and doing God's will.

GOSPEL: MATTHEW 5:13–20

The Gospel reading does not tell disciples to try to become the light of the world; they are that light (Matt. 5:14). The implications of vv. 15–16 may suggest that followers could hide or dim that light, but that does not take away from the awareness that the coming of the kingdom and its vocation have made them to be this light.

As with other portions of his Gospel, Matthew has evidently drawn the sayings in vv. 13–16 from his sources and then added to and/or developed the material. The saying of v. 15 about a lamp not meant to be put under a bushel is also found twice in Luke (8:16; 11:33) and Mark (4:21). In Mark it has to do with the purpose of parables. One cannot, of course, be sure how Jesus may have originally intended it or whether he may have used the basic saying on more than one occasion. Perhaps it once was more directly related to the inbreaking of the kingdom and the proclamation of its coming. Matthew sees the community of disciples not as having replaced the kingdom, but as being its light or beacon. The evangelist is not, however, entirely happy with the present-day disciples. His Gospel is written for what has been called a "mixed community." He several times alludes to those who are called as a mixture of good and bad, wheat and weeds (e.g., Matt. 13:24–30, 47–50; 22:10; 25:31–46). The sorting out will come at the end, but Matthew is meanwhile concerned about laxness and lack of zeal within the community. The saying on salt (see Luke 14:34–35; Mark 9:50) seems to suggest this and carries with it a warning.

How exactly the bold images of salt and light are intended is not clear. Matthew has linked the sayings to the disciples who are reviled and persecuted (vv. 11–12). We know also that he has in mind the mission of the church to all the world. Some would today counsel us that if the church is to have anything significant to say to the world it must first be what it was meant to be. The church cannot, for example, tell the world how to avoid war, if the church itself is full of strife. By keeping their own lights shining clearly and purifying their lives together Christians may become beacon lights of hope and saltiness to others. Matthew, however, seems also to see the dangers involved in trying to become a pure remnant community. Being the light "of the world" and the "salt of the earth" and having a mission to preach, teach, serve, and baptize seem in this Gospel also to demand a more open, inclusive, and risking attitude to the world. It is a tension every Christian group must live with.

How does the community continue to be salty and to shine brightly? Some might think it can be done without the guidance of the law. They would even oppose gospel to law. Members of Matthew's audience may have been aware of interpretations of Paul's teaching, or have thought that Matthew or Jesus was suggesting that the law had been superseded. Perhaps some Jews accused Christians of teaching that the law was no longer valid. Matthew's answer is more complex. The law and the prophets (i.e., the whole of the Jewish revelation), this Gospel seems to say, continues to have a critical and indispensable role. It expresses God's will and its purpose will be accomplished. The teaching of Jesus, however (perhaps especially in the following six antitheses, "You have heard that it was said . . . but I say to you"), rightly interprets this purpose and the true spirit of the law and prophets. The religious and ethical practices of many of the Pharisees were among the most disciplined and genuinely sacrificial the world has ever seen. But it is not by more law or a new law that one exceeds the righteousness of the scribes and Pharisees but by doing the will of God on the basis of Jesus' understanding. The negative effort to live righteously by avoiding evil must be replaced by the desire to do good (as Matt. 5:38–48 makes clear; see the Seventh Sunday after the Epiphany).

EPISTLE: 1 CORINTHIANS 2:1–11

We remember that Paul was concerned with divisions within the Corinthian community. In I Cor. 1:17 he maintains that his special vocation is "to preach the gospel, and not with eloquent wisdom, lest the cross of Christ be emptied of its power." Verses 18–30 then reflect on Christian wisdom and power found in Christ Jesus as contrasted to the wisdom and power of the world. In 2:1–5 Paul now recalls his first visit to Corinth and how he was with them "in much fear and trembling" (v. 3). It would be helpful to us as preachers if we could better understand Paul's meaning here. On the one hand, there are these passages and others (see 2 Cor. 10:10; 11:6) that suggest that Paul did not measure up to the Corinthians' expectations of oratorical ability. On the other hand, his speech is convincing and demonstrative in its spiritual power (1 Cor. 2:4). When Paul berates the Galatians (3:1) "before whose eyes Jesus Christ was publicly portrayed as crucified," he may well be referring to his preaching.

It is possible that when Paul speaks of the powerful presence of the Spirit, he may be thinking of the signs and wonders that he elsewhere reminds his hearers have accompanied his preaching (see 2 Cor. 12:12; Rom. 15:18–19), but it sounds as if he means a spiritual presence in the words as well. Paul is most likely making a distinction between his own plain, though in its way forceful, presentation of the gospel message and presentations couched in a more schooled and polished rhetorical style. The art of rhetoric or persuasion had been highly developed in several Hellenistic centers, and it is possible that Paul is still attacking the "I belong to Apollos" group (1 Cor. 1:12) with its probable concern with allegorical method and rhetorical skill and, perhaps, also with a tendency to deemphasize the powerlessness and evident folly by worldly standards of a crucified Christ. Paul's speech may not have met rhetorical standards of subtlety and that kind of persuasiveness, but this enabled the Corinthians' faith to be based on the power of God in the message and not in the cleverness of the preacher.

Today we might think in terms of advertising or packaging being at least as potentially dangerous to the true power of the gospel message. How do we respond when someone tells us that our preaching would be much more effective if we made better use of the techniques of modern advertising? Supposing we did and many came to hear us?

How do we best tell people of Christ? Who are the great preachers? I remember being surprised in my seminary preaching class to learn that some of the great preachers of my Anglican tradition (John Henry Newman, Philips Brooks, F. W. Robertson) were not that gifted by our contemporary standards when it came to public-speaking styles. It was substance and, perhaps above all, who they were as believing Christians that allowed the Spirit to speak through them.

Verses 6–11 go on to tell of a wisdom that mature Christians can claim to have—not one known in the world at large nor by "the rulers of this age," a reference both to earthly *powers that be* and the supernatural forces that stand behind them. It is the Spirit of God which is to God, Paul suggests, as the reflective mind or spirit is to humans, that makes true wisdom known. This is an analogy worth pondering. That which enables us to be spiritual beings is our ability to think about our thinking and be in dialogue with self. God, as it were, has this self-awareness, too, God's Spirit, and with this Spirit our self-awareness can have a further relationship. (Further on 1 Cor. 2:6–11, see next Sunday's commentary.)

The Sixth Sunday after the Epiphany

Lutheran	Roman Catholic	Episcopal	Common Lectionary
Deut. 30:15–20	Sir. 15:15–20	Sir. 15:11–20	Deut. 30:15–20 or Ecclus. 15:15–20
1 Cor. 2:6–13	1 Cor. 2:6–10	1 Cor. 3:1–9	1 Cor. 3:1–9
Matt. 5:20–37	Matt. 5:17–37	Matt. 5:21–24, 27–30, 33–37	Matt. 5:17–26

In many ethical discussions we may find ourselves torn between wanting to insist that there are right and wrong standards of behavior, which must not be obscured by too much debate about particular circumstances, and, on the other hand, recognizing that laws enunciated without any sensitivity for individual situations and changing conditions may come to seem both legalistic and inhuman. Preachers who would like to stir up some vigorous and even painful reflection need only read the Gospel lesson and ask a few questions of themselves, their people, and modern mores.

FIRST LESSON: DEUTERONOMY 30:15–20

Both the reading from Deuteronomy and the Ecclesiasticus lesson listed in other lectionaries provide important insights and valuable background material for this discussion. Deuteronomy 30:15–20 concludes a speech made by Moses (Deuteronomy 29—30) in the land of Moab before the people crossed into the promised land.

The covenant he speaks of is a kind of renewal of the original Sinai covenant. While the speech makes use of language that could reach back to the time of the historical Moses, it was composed at a later date, perhaps as a preparation for the return from exile (see 30:1–10). It is based on ideas developed during the Deuteronomic reform under King Josiah. The speech sets forth the history of the covenant relationship, reminding the people of God's mighty acts and the Lord's promise if they are obedient. The text (30:11–14) insists that the covenant demand is not beyond human comprehension or capacity. "The word is very near you; it is in your mouth and heart so that you can do it" (v. 14). The speech then concludes with a stark description of the two ways between which Israel must choose. These verses could have been used as part of a covenant ceremony such as is found in Deut. 26:16—27:26 and Josh. 24:14–27.

The words "life" and "to live," repeated through vv. 15–20, mean the continued life of the people and a quality of life which is "good." The words "good" and evil" in v. 15 are used not in a moral sense, but to mean "well-being" contrasted with grave difficulties and suffering. Verse 16 refers to what seems to be many commandments, statutes, and ordinances, but the emphasis is on keeping the Torah, which, the people have just been told, is not beyond their reach. This is, in fact, chiefly done by "Loving the Lord your God," that is, by worshiping the Lord alone as God and not the other gods of the land (v. 17).

In modern dress the temptation to love other gods may come in the various ways people experience difficulty in keeping the purposes and will of God first in their lives. There are many guises or disguises under which they can find themselves worshiping some other goal or god such as wealth, fame, power, or even survival, health, and family as coequal with or above the God of all. We may also want to maintain that God wills some of these good things for humanity and that they need not be opposed to the purposes of God. This can well be true, but not if they become substitute gods that primarily determine who we are and what we do.

Some contemporary theologians tend to balk at the idea that God should reward and bless with the good things of life those who love and obey God. Should not service and love of God be their own reward? Is love genuine and a spirit of service true if done only to get a reward? These are appropriate questions to ask of this passage, but it should also be recognized that, while we can never be sure that individual lives given to God will escape calamity and suffering, communities of people that care for one another and whose members live upright lives do often prosper in

the world. In this sense a charitable and just people may be said to find
their reward.

ALTERNATIVE FIRST LESSON: ECCLESIASTICUS 15:15–20

This lection takes up another aspect of the moral life. The section begins
with vv. 11–12, and with those who see the Lord as responsible for human
failures and sins. One theological perspective has held from this time
through our own that God is in charge of everything. If God is in charge,
then God must have made the evil in us as well as the good. How can we
be responsible? The contemporary secular version would bring to bear
sociological and psychological theories of determinism. These should not
be dismissed lightly. Maybe one feels free at the present moment to do
this or to do that, but, looking back on life, it is possible to see that many
choices were in fact pretty much determined by circumstances, upbringing,
custom, what was "expected of us," and so forth.

Are human beings in some sense *free*? Are they morally responsible
agents? While insisting on God's omniscience, this lection maintains that
they are and echoes (v. 17) the sharp choice of Deut. 30:15–20. Contemporary ethical discussion must, however, recognize the limits of human
freedom and responsibility. But, once that is done, it becomes possible
also to recognize the awesome and mysterious capacity of human beings—
not just to think—but to think about their thinking, and so in some measure
to transcend their immediate circumstances and gain at least a degree of
choice. With this freedom also comes, sometimes painfully, responsibility,
as Ecclesiasticus reminds us.

GOSPEL: MATTHEW 5:21–37

The first of Jesus' radical interpretations of the law (Matt. 5:21–48) is
presented in vv. 21–24 and the thrust of these verses rightly reminds hearers
of Isaiah 58 (see last Sunday's reading) and the passionate concern of other
prophets for a genuine and reconciled community of Israel. The driving
motivation of much of Jesus' ministry may have been to prepare a restored,
inclusive community for the coming of the kingdom. The note of urgency
is heard especially in vv. 23–24, as is also the insight that reconciliation
with others in the community is a prerequisite for the worship of God.
One thinks back to Isaiah and also ahead to Matt. 6:14–15 where knowing
God's forgiveness is said to require the disciples' willingness to forgive.

With the commandment not to kill (Exod. 20:13; Deut. 5:17), Jesus
goes directly to the Ten Commandments and the heart of the written law.
Individuals might claim that they had never killed anyone and so kept the
law in this regard. Much more is involved, Jesus teaches, in living up to
the purpose and spirit of the law. One must not even attack a person's basic

dignity for such can deprive them of their place in the community, their sense of worth and thus be worse than killing them.

In setting up gradations of crimes with their punishments, Jesus may have been depending on knowledge of ways of dealing with culpability such as are found at Qumran, particularly in "The Manual of Discipline." But, perhaps partly as hyperbole to make the point, he seems to invert the order; as the crimes appear to become lesser, the punishments grow more fierce. Whoever kills is liable to "judgment," (i.e., what is coming to them under the law, but perhaps also with reference to the judgment of God). But even one who is angry with a community member deserves as much, while the one who says *raca* (an Aramaic insult of some kind) is liable to the Sanhedrin (the highest court in the land). Finally, someone who calls another community member a "fool" (Greek = *mōre,* related to our word "moron") is liable to the Gehenna of fire (i.e., the final and irremediable punishment).

Hyperbole may be involved, but the intent is very serious. Every preacher and congregation will be challenged when they ask how they today may, by their words or actions, vilify and dehumanize others. One may think of racial slurs and jokes, but every act of sneering and trying to set others outside the community of basic respect and equality can come into conscience.

Jesus' words about lust and adultery assume freedom and responsibility (recall the discussion of Ecclus. 15:15–20), though at least part of us will again want to raise questions. How free are we, for example, not to lust? The sexual drive and attraction to others is powerfully instilled in all animals. It is how the species continues. When one adds to this drive human insecurities, loneliness, and the desire to be loved and to love, one has some strong chemistry that is not easy to turn off or direct at will. One should probably assume, however, that the demand of Jesus' ethic has taken human nature into account, perhaps in some ways better than we normally do. One recognizes, in the first place, that the saying deals with lust and not simply desire or sexual urge. Lust is what is done with that desire. One has some choice as to whether desire will be recognized and then put in its proper place, or whether it will be entertained and have a party held for it. One also recognizes that the words about lust in the heart are said to be the equivalent of adultery, which indicates *lusting* or *coveting* after another's wife. (The Greek words here and in the Greek translation of "You shall not covet your neighbor's wife" in Exod. 20:17 and Deut. 5:21 are the same: *epithumeō.*) While it would probably be a mistake to focus the spirit of this saying too narrowly, its main concern is with the damage of lustful thoughts in relation to the commitments of marriage.

The warning is reinforced by exaggerated advice about what to do with parts of the body that may become involved in sinning. If followed literally, most of us would end up as blind, deaf, and speechless quadriplegics. But this hyperbolic language is meant to reinforce the seriousness of Jesus' interpretation of the law about adultery. The new life of the kingdom calls for a radical purity. Some scholars have suggested that the ethical challenge put forth by Jesus is so demanding that it must be viewed as an attempt to make everyone aware that they cannot live up to the law and are desperately in need of God's saving grace. Others hold that Jesus taught an "interim ethic" (i.e., an ethic that could be sustained only in the short period between the proclamation of the coming reign of God and its consummation). It would not fully apply to normal human circumstances.

One cannot, of course, surely know Jesus' or Matthew's intention, but the major thrust of the six antitheses in Matt. 5:21–48 seems to expect the possibility of changed relationships based on a transformed human motivation in the light of the coming kingdom. In our passage this expectation is then extended into the always difficult area of divorce. Here Jesus' words need to be heard in the context of a debate among his contemporaries. One school claimed that a man could only divorce his wife for some act of unchastity, based on a word usually translated as "unseemly" or "indecency" in the Pentateuch's teaching about divorce (Deut. 24:1–4). But another school of teachers claimed that a cause for divorce could involve anything that displeased a husband, from bad looks to bad cooking to talking too much. Jesus' saying in Matt. 5:32 (see also Matt. 19:9) seems to side with the stricter school, though it is often thought (since "except for unchastity" is not found in Mark 10:11 or Luke 16:18) that Matthew or his tradition has added the exception in order to help the church apply the teaching as a rule to deal with complex human circumstances.

The preacher who wants to use these sayings to help involve the congregation in serious reflection on sexuality and marriage is probably best advised to try to dig deeply into their significance. (This method can be said to be a more *fundamental* approach to Scripture than some form of literalistic, surface interpretation.) Jesus would seem to encourage this attitude in his major teaching on marriage (Matt. 19:3–9; Mark 10:2–10) when he sets the marriage relationship in the context of God's purpose in creation. What God intended, Jesus may have maintained, is no divorce. There is no getting around this understanding by human laws or rulings.

But what then should be said when people who began marriage with this understanding find that their relationship has disintegrated and become harmful to themselves and perhaps to others? Were Jesus' words meant to be a new law on this subject? Or is this to be seen as part of an impossible interim ethic which an ongoing body of Christians, much less an ongoing society, cannot hope fully to live up to and follow?

Or, once the church has used Jesus' teaching with the utmost seriousness to understand the sacredness and responsibility of marriage, might it not be called to apply his words as the principle on marriage for its members rather than a new piece of law? (He certainly does not seem to have been concerned with creating new laws in other areas.) Christian communities might best employ their energies to support all marriages, using the principle to guard against any form of casual divorce, but not to prevent the recognition that some marriages fail and the individuals need to be supported in new circumstances and possible new marriages undertaken in trust in God's forgiveness and care.

It is sometimes thought that Jesus' main concern in this regard may have been to protect women who were largely defenseless in the marriage relationship in his society. The brunt of the saying is then not intended so much to offer a general law about marriage as it is directed against men who would cast off their wives. This may help us understand why it is said in Matt. 5:32 that the divorce would make the former wife an adulteress. She would have to get married again to survive. Throughout all Jesus' challenging teaching about sexuality there is heard the demand that women not be treated as objects of gratification or as property. In the new community there is to be a new quality of relationship between men and women.

In a different context of human affairs the character and quality of relationships can be heard as the major concern of the following antithesis, vv. 33–37. In Jesus' time and culture the vows and promises people made had more importance than they do now. Much of daily life depended on a person's word, for there were not as many written contracts, records, and lawyers to help deal with those who would go back on their word. Three important passages from the Pentateuch—Lev. 19:12; Num. 30:2; Deut. 23:21–23—describe the seriousness and significance of vows somewhat as Matt. 23:16–22 does from a particular perspective. James 5:12 contains an admonition similar to Matt. 5:33–37, and it is sometimes thought to be, at least in part, an earlier version of the Matthean teaching. The saying seems to counsel that people not lightly use God's name or things related to the worship of God in oaths and that they be straightforward and open in their promises and vows. That is all that is necessary. One might ponder the degree to which our many written contracts and legalities have today inclined us to be a society that confuses what is right with what is legally enforceable. Is one only obligated to fulfill a promise when it can be proven that it was made and made under enforceable legal circumstances? What contemporary incidents can be used to illustrate this concern?

EPISTLE: 1 CORINTHIANS 2:6–13

Since some lectionaries use 1 Cor. 2:6–11 as a portion of last Sunday's reading, vv. 6–13 were briefly discussed in our previous section. The verses present a kind of paradox to both past and present hearers of Paul's message. He had been telling the Corinthians that wisdom, as they were understanding it, was not a special philosophy that some Christians had gained. Particularly concerned with divisions in the Corinthian community, Paul radically contrasted the message about the crucified Christ to worldly ideas of wisdom and power. His proclamation of the Gospel had not been offered to them in the persuasive rhetoric of wisdom but in spiritual power (2:1–5).

Now, however, Paul contends, there can be said to be a wisdom known only to Christians—imparted, in fact, only to the mature *(teleioi)*. *Teleioi* was used in some of the mystery religion cults of the time to designate a "perfected" class of believers, and it may be that Paul is making a two-pronged attack (as he does elsewhere). On the one hand, the kind of wisdom some Corinthians are claiming as a special possession is not of God, but, on the other hand, there is "a secret (or, "mysterious") and hidden wisdom of God," or one may translate "we impart a wisdom of God in a mystery" (v. 7). None of the "rulers of this age" *(archai tou aiōnos,* referring both to the Pilates, Herods, and Caiaphases of this world and the supernatural forces that give them their power) understood this wisdom, which may be the wisdom of God's plan of salvation or salvation itself or perhaps both.

While Paul's phraseology here offers a kind of corrected view of faith, using some of the words of certain of the Corinthians, one should also recognize the links of this language to Jewish apocalyptic thought. The apparent quotation in v. 9 (possibly influenced by Isa. 64:4 but perhaps drawn from an unknown intertestamental writing), along with vv. 10–12, suggest this context of the revelation of heavenly secrets. The preacher may want to take on the challenging task of trying to distinguish between contemporary forms of philosophy and wisdom which have little room for a suffering Christ and a spiritual wisdom based on the message of the crucified one.

Paul then goes on in vv. 14–16 and 3:1–9 (used today in the Common Lectionary) to distinguish between the type of individual who is unspiritual or only of the natural order *(psychikos)* and the spiritual *(pneumatikos)* to whom the Spirit of God (see last week's lection on the analogy of 2:10–12) can impart gifts. The Corinthians may have been criticizing Paul for (in contrast to Apollos) preaching too simple a gospel message. Paul says he had to be simple because they were still like children in the faith, as their jealousy and strife gave evidence. But the passage ends on an irenic note: both Paul and Apollos are but servants, fellow workers, who have planted and watered the one plant (3:5–8), and, switching analogies, "you are God's field, God's building" (v. 9).

The Seventh Sunday after the Epiphany

Lutheran	Roman Catholic	Episcopal	Common Lectionary
Lev. 19:1–2, 17–18	Lev. 19:1–2, 17–18	Lev. 19:1–2, 9–18	Isa. 49:8–12
1 Cor. 3:10–11, 16–23	1 Cor. 3:16–23	1 Cor. 3:10-11, 16-23	1 Cor. 3:10–11, 16–23
Matt. 5:38–48	Matt. 5:38–48	Matt. 5:38–48	Matt. 5:27–37*

*The Gospel lesson in the Common Lectionary for today is Matt. 5:27–37. For a commentary on this reading see the previous Sunday. The Common Lectionary uses Isa. 49:8–13 for its first lesson. Following on the second of the "servant songs," Isa. 49:1–6(7) (see The Second Sunday after the Epiphany), this dramatic reading repeats or echoes a number of themes found earlier in 2 Isaiah. It uses motifs of the exodus to tell of the people's return from exile and restoration. On the covenant in 49:8 see 42:6. On coming forth from prison and darkness (49:9) see 42:7. Verses 9c–11 are rich with language drawn from the exodus story and which is also found, e.g., in Isa. 40:3–4, 11; 48:20–22. The mention of "land" in v. 8 is of significance both for that time and today. Israel needs a place in order to be a people, a land that is newly apportioned among the needy. The passage closes with a hymnic response.

FIRST LESSON: LEVITICUS 19:1–2, 9–18
EPISTLE: 1 CORINTHIANS 3:10–11, 16–23
GOSPEL: MATTHEW 5:38–48

What is expected of God's people? How holy and loving are they to be? People ask such questions in the abstract. Books are written about the principles of ethics and justice. But the questions can also become very specific, especially when one feels wronged or people are concerned that their group is not getting their fair share or fair shake. What people often want then is some law or guideline setting down the limits of what or how much they are expected to endure or do before they can claim their own. Tell me, I ask, what I need to do in order to be an ethical person. This may sound as if I am motivated by a positive desire to do good, but what is prompting my question could well be a more negative concern with knowing when I have done enough. So the lawyer who asks Jesus, Who is my neighbor? may well be asking, Whom can I set outside my sphere of care without forfeiting my good conscience? Jesus responds with a story of a robbed and injured man who was helped by someone (a Samaritan in the heart of Judea) who had every right to claim, This is no neighbor of mine (Luke 10:25–37). How do efforts to set limits on neighbor love sound after experiencing such a parable?

Matthew 5:38–48 breathes the same spirit of the Jesus who told the parable of the good Samaritan, as well as stories about the father of the prodigal son and his hard-working elder brother, and about the all-day laborers in the vineyard jealous of the one-hour workers who were paid equally with them. The two antitheses, "You have heard that it was said . . . but I say to you," concluding the series of six such sayings begun at v. 21 press home to the still startled hearers what it means that "your righteousness exceed that of the scribes and Pharisees" (Matt. 5:20). With a love that is concerned not only for neighbors but for enemies, disciples are to "be perfect, as your heavenly father is perfect" (5:48).

Surely this is astounding counsel, though perhaps made too familiar by our repeated hearing of it. In many ways it is incredible. How can human beings be like God in their love? Our lives are dominated by so much self-centeredness if not selfishness. Together with advice that one turn the other cheek, go the extra mile, and give to the one who begs (vv. 39, 41–42), it may even seem like unwise counsel to those who know the moral maxim, "The best is the enemy of the good." Such perfection and altruism appear so far beyond human practice in the great majority of everyday, practical situations that the temptation is surely strong to give up the whole ethical enterprise or merely to sound pious about it, mouthing platitudes in church but really living by some other, often unexamined standards borrowed from the culture.

In somewhat different language the readings from 1 Corinthians and Leviticus seem to reinforce the outrageous character of the divine demand. Paul tells the new Christians that they are God's temple and that God's Spirit indwells them, and that "if anyone destroys God's temple, God will destroy that person" (1 Cor. 3:16–17; see also 2 Cor. 6:16, "We are the temple of the living God"). Disciples have now, as it were, replaced the sacredness of the holy temple and so, it is certainly implied, they are to treat one another. "You shall be holy; for I the Lord your God am holy" are the words that begin the holiness teaching of Leviticus 19, which is a kind of commentary on and application of the Ten Commandments. In matters of daily justice and charity, as well as in cultic practice, the standard of behavior is not set by human understandings of their ethical limits, but rather in relationship to the holiness of God. In the heart of the chapter (v. 18) the people are told, "You shall love your neighbor as yourself." The neighbor is a member of one's own group, but, in order to forestall inclinations to limit the requirement of love, one learns (v. 34) that "the stranger who sojourns with you shall be to you as the native among you, and you shall love the sojourner as yourself."

The opening words of Leviticus 19 offer a critical insight about holiness. Holiness is of God. It attaches to Israel, as it were, in the relationship with God. In this sense it is like the calling of the Corinthians to be "sanctified," "holy ones," "saints" (1 Cor. 1:2; see 2 Cor. 1:1). They are God's temple by God's action, not their own. God sets the people of God apart by the divine calling, and the call to be "perfect" can at least partially be understood in this way as well. God establishes the relationship through which disciples can be "perfected." One is reminded of the words of the Johannine disciple: "We love, because God first loved us" (1 John 4:19).

The word "Perfect" *(teleios)* needs careful translation. It means to come to the goal or purpose, that is, to become what one was created for, to reach full growth, potential, maturity. Ephesians 4:13 presents the vision of all Christians attaining "to the unity of the faith and of the knowledge of the Son of God, to mature *(teleios)* humanity, to the measure of the stature of the fullness of Christ." For humans to be perfect or fully grown as ethical persons means to be so in their own human order.

Recognition of the human order of the perfection to which disciples are called must not, however, take away from the moral mystery of what it means to become holy and to "be perfect as your heavenly Father is perfect." We always want to set limits, but the point of Matt. 5:48 may be that, in relationship with God, there are no limits on who we may become morally and ethically. The way is open once we recognize the relationship with God and God's calling. It is important to realize that we are beginners in the moral life—people in need of understanding, forgiveness, and new beginnings. But we may also see ourselves as people just beginning to recognize the power of love that is God's gift. We become who we are meant to be—God's children—as we more maturely reflect the character of the divine parent.

Leviticus 19:3–8 comments on the first half of the Decalogue, vv. 9–22 on the second half. While Leviticus 17–26 (the so-called Holiness Code) was finally composed after the exile, it is drawn from reflection reaching well back into Israel's history as a covenant people. The refrain "I am the Lord" or "I am the Lord your God," repeated twelve times through Leviticus 19, reminds the people to whom they belong and of the God calling them to be holy. Being "holy" means they are to be consecrated and set apart from all that is profane, although the detailed regulations of life following the Torah begin then to work in the other direction, toward consecrating all of life.

Verses 9–10 tell farmers to leave something of their crop for the poor and sojourner (foreign hired workers, somewhat like our migrant workers). Verses 11–12 summarize the commandments not to steal, deal or swear falsely, or to lie. Verses 13–14 have to do with the protection of workers and the handicapped. Verses 15–16 speak particularly to the responsibilities of all citizens with respect to the local councils of justice. Justice requires impartiality with regard to community standing and wealth. Verse 16 is difficult to translate with precision. It apparently means that one should not in a vengeful manner tell tales about one's own people nor do something that would put the life of one's neighbor in jeopardy when a capital charge is involved. A person should not, in other words, give false evidence or testify lightly.

A strong echo of Lev. 19:17a is heard in Matt. 5:21–22. Not nursing hatred against kin is similar to the warning against being angry with or belittling one of one's own people. Leviticus 19:17b seems to suggest that an individual must be ready to reprove a neighbor when the neighbor is guilty of some sin (see Matt. 18:15–17) so that one will not bear responsibility for the sin. Both halves of Lev. 19:18 are taken up in the Gospel reading. The counsel not to take vengeance seems to be at the heart of Matt. 5:38–39.

The ancient *lex talionis* (law of retaliation) in Matt. 5:38 (see Exod. 21:22–25; Lev. 24:19–20; Deut. 19:16–21) seems originally to have been designed to curb unrestrained vengeance. In one sense, it may sound merciless ("You knock out my tooth, and yours will be knocked out"), but such a law is better than killing people for breaking a tooth or maiming someone. Jesus' interest goes deeper, into the profound and complex issue of responding to evil. Every moral person must struggle with such concerns. How does one deal with an unfair neighbor, with criminals, with terrorists? Is it Jesus' teaching that the only way to stop evil is to absorb it rather than pass it on? What do we teach the child whom we spank for hitting her brother? What do we teach society by killing murderers? What is the basic motivation of our criminal justice system? How can we halt the cycle of terrorism?

Paul wrote, "Repay no one evil for evil . . . never avenge yourselves." Disciples are to feed and give drink to enemies so shaming them. "Do not be overcome by evil, but overcome evil with good" (Rom. 12:17–21). Martin Luther King, Jr. said to his oppressors, "We shall match your capacity to inflict suffering by our capacity to endure suffering. . . . But be ye assured that we will wear you down by our capacity to suffer. One day we shall win freedom, but not only for ourselves. We shall so appeal to your heart and conscience that we shall win you in the process, and our victory will be a double victory" (*Strength to Love* [Philadelphia: Fortress Press, 1981], 54–55).

This double victory could have been Jesus' intention as well, but he does not say that good will come of absorbing evil. He says it is to be done, and no hearer of the Gospels' teaching can forget that Jesus did not just say such things but enacted them in response to his own persecution.

An Austrian newspaper reporter was betrayed to the Nazis by a colleague in 1939. Imprisoned all through the war, he survived by nursing his hatred and sense of revenge. Finally, two years after the war, he spotted his betrayer on a street in Vienna. He walked toward him—but then passed him by, saying to himself, "This has to stop somewhere."

One hears Desmond Tutu insisting to P. W. Botha that he is his brother and that they are of the same human family. The preacher may wish to ask who we regard as enemies and how they can be loved.

Despite such stories an aura of moral dilemma will not go away. What do you do with the crazed individual who keeps hitting you on the other side of the face? Or what do you do when someone is beating someone else? It is one thing to ask ourselves to absorb the evil of an aggressor nation. What do we do when that nation is slaughtering others? Are Christians meant to be absolute pacifists? Nonviolent resisters of evil? Ready to fight in a "just" war?

The hard questions persist. Perhaps all one can say with some certainty is that the motive of revenge is forbidden to disciples. Jesus drives home this demanding and, in its way, almost impossible message: *Never strike back in revenge.*

There follow three other illustrations of how far Christians should be willing to go. The next two seem more closely related to the theme of not resisting one who is evil. When disciples are sued for their "suit" or "dress" (the basic sleeved garment of the time), they should give up their cloak or outer garment as well. (Exod. 22:26; Deut. 24:10, 12–13 speak specifically to the creditors who would take a neighbor's or a poor person's cloak.) "If anyone forces you to go a mile" (a practice used by the occupying Romans to make the locals help them with their burdens), "go two." Here again, the disciples are to respond by going beyond what law (see Exod. 22:25; Lev. 25:35–37) or custom would require.

Most of us would like to lead our lives in such a way that we become neither victimizers of others nor victims. Jesus' words seem to suggest that, when forced to choose, disciples should be victims.

The law of Lev. 19:18 certainly does not say that God's people are to hate their enemies while loving neighbors, but Jesus' words probably refer to popular interpretation. Although many Jews strove to extend the law of love to non-Jews, throughout their history they had known times of hatred, of enemies from the Egyptians to the Amalekites to the Romans. The Dead Sea Scroll, "The Manual of Discipline," says that God has commanded the saints to hate all that God has despised (1:4) . . . all the sons of darkness (1:10)." Especially in times of war and persecution, most peoples have found it very difficult not to hate their enemies and often to claim that it is God's will that they do so. Psalm 139:21–22 catches that fierce spirit well:

> Do I not hate them that hate thee, O Lord?
> And do I not loathe them that rise against thee?
> I hate them with perfect hatred;
> I count them my enemies.

Jesus tells of a different will of God and so a different way of life for those who would be children of this God and reflect their parent's character. God is extraordinarily evenhanded with divine providence. In some ways Matt. 5:45 is the most surprising and even shocking statement in the Bible. It seems to run counter to much that is said elsewhere about God blessing the good and at least not blessing if not punishing evil. But it is a fact that nature seems to make no distinction, and Jesus draws a lesson that seems consonant with the surprising gracefulness of God that he alludes to in several of his parables.

Luke's parallel (Luke 6:36) to Matt. 5:36 reads, "Be merciful, even as your Father is merciful," which is an easier counsel to comprehend and in some ways better concludes the teaching of this lesson and the whole of Matthew 5. But Matthew's "You, therefore, must be perfect . . . ," sets out the challenge and the invitation to an unlimited human adventure in holiness.

We remember that Paul has been deeply concerned with divisions in the Corinthian church, and especially with a tendency on the part of some to boast that they have a special wisdom (sophia) that sets them apart. In the course of this discussion Paul insists that neither he nor any of the other church leaders should be seen as more than servants through whom "God gave the growth" (1 Cor. 3:6–7). Verses 10–23, and especially vv. 18–23, tie up the threads of this discussion, with vv. 22–23 referring directly back to 1:12.

Picking up the image of God's building in 1 Cor. 3:9, Paul pictures himself as a skilled or wise (sophos) master builder, but the foundation he lays is Jesus Christ. The thrust of Paul's understanding of his ministry is stated still more directly in 2 Cor. 4:5. "What we preach is not ourselves, but Jesus Christ as Lord, with ourselves as your servants for Jesus' sake." There is no boasting (3:21; see 1:29, 31; 4:7; Rom. 3:27; Eph. 2:9). True wisdom, which knows the power of the crucified Lord, is a gift of God. The wisdom of this world and this age (*aiōn,* with the nuance that it is "this passing age"), based on its own ideas of what is strong, lasting, and important, is folly with God. Paul quotes Job 5:13 and Ps. 94:11 to illustrate God's disparagement of human forms of wisdom. The preacher will be challenged at this point to find examples of worldly wisdom that illustrate such folly but do not simply lead to praise of irrationality and derision of the God-given human intellect.

The passage closes on a positive, hymnic note—more akin to 1 Cor. 1:2–9 than what has intervened. Verse 21b may represent a play on a Stoic aphorism: "All things belong to the wise one." Because, Paul tells the Corinthians, "all things are yours," there is no point in divisions. Verse 23 presents Paul's christological insight that "you are of Christ, and Christ is of God" (see also 1 Cor. 15:28). Although in one sense this subordinates Christ to God, in another way it leads toward the understanding that the Lordship of Christ is the Lordship of the one God.

The Eighth Sunday after the Epiphany

Lutheran	Roman Catholic	Episcopal	Common Lectionary
Isa. 49:13–18	Isa. 49:14–15	Isa. 49:8–18	Lev. 19:1–2, 9–18
1 Cor. 4:1–13	1 Cor. 4:1–5	1 Cor. 4:1–5, 8–13	1 Cor. 4:1–5
Matt. 6:24–34	Matt. 6:24–34	Matt. 6:24–34	Matt. 5:38–48*

*For commentary on Lev. 19:1–2, 9–18 and Matt. 5:38–48 see The Seventh Sunday after the Epiphany.

Don't worry, we tell ourselves and others. Sometimes this counsel is accompanied by Stoic advice in the form of a rhetorical question: What can you do about it? Perhaps less often today people are told not to worry because their trust can be in God. Sometimes Don't worry is a little more than a friendly good wish to which is added, It will probably turn out all right. Yet we keep on worrying. Anxiety seems to dominate much of modern life, and many see it growing as life's pace picks up and technology and the information explosion offer people more and more options. Indeed, they worry about all the anxiety in the world. Maybe we all worry that we worry too much and that it affects our health and our relationships.

While it seems foolish to worry about things we cannot change, still we manage to do it. I am over fifty years old but still fret that I am not taller. Whether the rhetorical question of Matthew's (6:27) was intended to admonish against anxiety about adding a cubit (literally about eighteen inches, the length of a forearm) to one's height or the span of one's life, the advice speaks to me. In his well-known prayer used by Alcoholics Anonymous, Reinhold Niebuhr asks, "God grant me the serenity to accept the things I cannot change, the courage to change the things I can, and the wisdom to distinguish the one from the other." Yet, even in those times when I find the wisdom for such discernment, I find that there are still many aspects of life about which to be anxious.

FIRST LESSON: ISAIAH 49:13–18

In their different ways today's three readings all speak to the condition of human anxiety. The passage from Isaiah begins on a note of exultation. The exile has come to an end, and the Lord has comforted the people. But then (48:14) the voice of human doubt and worry breaks in: Look at all the evidence on the other side. How can the Lord care? Zion (i.e., the people of Jerusalem located on Mt. Zion) said, "The Lord has forsaken me; my Lord has forgotten me." The response of God is one of the Bible's most moving passages. "Can a woman forget the infant at the breast, being without compassion for the child of her womb?" The question is basically rhetorical, but at least it is conceivable that some mother might forget her child. But not God. There is an ancient Celtic saying, "There is a mother's heart in the heart of God," and one thinks of other biblical passages, such as Isa. 66:13, that tell of God's compassion and care in strong maternal imagery.

In another image (v. 16) the name Zion (or perhaps a drawing of the rebuilt city) is said to be engraved on the caring hands of God. There may be an allusion here to a Babylonian custom of tattooing the name of one's god on the hand, a custom with which those returning from exile would be familiar (see also Exod. 13:9). But here God, as it were, makes a tattoo of God's people. A Christian thinks ahead to the wounds on the hands of the crucified Savior. The hands by which we will be judged have holes in their palms.

A little later in Isaiah 49 (vv. 20–21) the language of maternal care is used again, this time of Zion. The city has been desolate and bereaved, but now the place will seem too small for all her inhabitants. Like a mother with too many children, she will wonder where they all have come from. Through the eyes of God and with God's words the prophet is even now able to picture the new city as it is being finished. The rebuilders (v. 17) will do their work even more quickly than those who destroyed it. The many returning inhabitants will be like a bride's jewels ornamenting the rebuilt city.

EPISTLE: 1 CORINTHIANS 4:1–5

In the opening chapters of 1 Corinthians, Paul has been trying to reduce Corinthian anxieties about belonging to the right group and having enough wisdom. In some ways certain of the Corinthians may seem fairly confident about these matters, but it is human nature to boast about what one is most insecure about. The closing verses of last Sunday's reading (3:21–23) reassure the Corinthians that all things that really count are theirs, given to them as a gift of God. They are God's temple (3:16–17).

Now Paul comes again to his role in the ministry of salvation. This teaching is directed to the Corinthians to help them understand how he and all Christian leaders should be regarded, but it is not difficult also to hear Paul speaking to some of his own anxieties. All who are given roles of leadership in the church will have known some of his thoughts and feelings and will want to ponder his words.

Questions about his role were never far from Paul's mind and come up repeatedly in his correspondence. They were already discussed in this letter in 1:1, 13–17; 2:1–5; 3:1–15. Most ministers are sensitive to other people's criticism and views of them. Paul, whatever his protestations to the contrary, was certainly no exception, and it does seem that the Corinthians had a fair number of criticisms regarding his customs, his speech, his presence, perhaps his lack of "wisdom" and accompanying rhetorical skill, and his failure to visit them as promised (see 1 Cor. 9:3–23; 2 Cor. 1:17–20; 10:10–12; 11:5–6).

Paul's (self-) advice is that human judgments count for little or nothing (4:3) for those who are "servants of Christ and stewards of the mysteries of God" (4:1). The words translated as "servants" *(hyperetai)* and "stewards" *(oikonomoi)* suggest people in subordinate but not inferior positions. *Hyperetai* was a word used of galley rowers but had come to refer to official witnesses and assistants in the law courts and public service. Today, it might best be translated "assistants." "Stewards" often managed considerable properties, but what they managed was not their own. This is the point of both analogies. "Assistants" and "stewards" serve at the behest and pleasure of their master. Their chief responsibility (v. 2) is to be trustworthy in this regard. Other people can criticize them all they want, but it is their master who judges them. Paul will be judged by God regarding his stewardship "of the mysteries of God" (4:1), that is, God's plan of salvation through the crucified Christ which extends to all Gentiles. The word "mysteries" may also carry an allusion to the *mysteries* of pagan mystery religions and the belief that Christians have something far better.

Disciples cannot, of course, entirely escape the need to make judgments of various kinds about others, and, by the time of chap. 5 of this letter, Paul will certainly be engaged in that activity. Such judgments, however, can only be provisional, and Paul would argue that, since it is the judgment of God alone that matters, "assistants" and "stewards" should have them in the right perspective.

Another source of anxiety can be self-criticism and judgment, but, again, this is of no real account. Paul has nothing on his "conscience" or that he is "aware of" (v. 4). The word *(synoida, syneidēsis)* does not connote the same degree of introspection or an inner accusing voice that it does to many modern Western ears. It is the knowledge of things done wrong, and Paul here and elsewhere displays a relatively robust "conscience" in this regard. In large measure this is because of his strong sense of God's justification. But, once more, it is not up to "assistants" and "stewards" to judge their own performance. "It is the Lord who judges me" (v. 4).

Paul then speaks (v. 5) of that judgment in apocalyptically flavored language. On the one hand, one must not "pronounce judgment before the time" *(kairos)* as perhaps some Corinthians thought they could do, claiming that the kingdom had already come for them in the Spirit. But, on the other hand, for Paul that time is not far off when the things hidden in darkness will be brought to light (see also Matt. 10:26; Luke 12:2; Mark 4:22; Luke 8:17) and when inner thoughts and motives will be disclosed (see Rom. 2:16). Then everyone will receive the praise they deserve from God.

GOSPEL: MATTHEW 6:24–34

We could give this Matthean lesson the superscription "Getting One's Priorities Straight." If one's priorities are right, there need be no anxiety. How does one set priorities straight? (1) Choose between the service of God and of material goods and wealth. (2) Have trust in God's provision of the necessities of life. (3) Seek first the kingdom of God. (4) Then, don't worry about tomorrow. All this, of course, is much easier said than done.

It has been maintained that one could fairly well describe another person by looking over their check register. It would tell of their interests, their obligations, their passions, their priorities. One could probably do a similar analysis of a community's or a nation's budget. Those of us who are Christians try to serve God and want to put the purposes and activity of God, the reign of God and God's "righteousness" (Matt. 6:33, an important Matthean emphasis in these chapters; 5:6, 10, 20), first in our lives. We recognize that if this can be done, other aspects of life that we value can have their rightful place. Indeed, we can rejoice in them as part of God's creation and goodness. Yet so many Christians have painfully—either slowly or perhaps in one awful shock of recognition—come to realize how hard this is to do.

The response of some Christians has been to establish the priority of God and the kingdom by denying the things of this world. Poverty, fasting, asceticism, chastity, mortification, and other acts of self-denial have been practiced. Often, however, it is the most self-denying who have discovered how deep sin runs, finding a kind of pride in their mortification that can come to be worshiped alongside of or before God.

Other Christians have taken a more world-affirming attitude. The goods of this world can be accepted and enjoyed as long as one worships God above all and uses money and material things rightly—by helping others and not for immoral or unworthy purposes. Right living, honest gain and investment, stewardship, tithing, and charity would be read about in the check registers of such individuals and families. Few would claim, however, that they are not involved in a constant struggle, and that in both overt and subtle ways mammon (from an Aramaic word meaning property, material things) does not make its claims upon them. One can try to make the choice between God and mammon firmly once in a lifetime but, in reality, it has to be made again and again. Whether or not one agrees with the contention that "the love of money is the root of all evil," it has to be recognized that "it is through this craving that some have wandered away from the faith and pierced their hearts with many pangs" (1 Tim. 6:10; see also Luke 16:9–13 on "unrighteous mammon" and the right use of it).

Along with making the decision between God and mammon comes opportunity to put the things of this world in perspective by not being anxious about them. The references to the natural world and to God's provision in Matt. 6:25–32 have led to a lot of romanticism and no little excusing of drifting and lazy life-styles, sometimes dependent upon others for daily bread. Indeed, one can quickly become critical of these thoughts. One can look at the natural world and see that it is dog eat dog as well as bountiful and beautiful—that the ones who don't worry about next winter and scurry about do not survive.

Probably, however, the Jesus who told the parable of the sower and what happened to many of the seeds in that story (Matt. 13:4–7) knew nature's complexity. He knew that people starved. But he probably also knew that much starvation is not the result of lack of food but is caused by maldistribution, by greed born of anxiety even among those with plenty. "There is enough for everyone's need, but not enough for everyone's greed," contended Mahatma Gandhi. The point of Jesus' illustrations has to do with overall trust in God and helping one put God before mammon, not with a thorough description of the natural world.

The Greek word *merimnaō* means "to care," but it often comes to mean to be overly concerned, to have anxiety. It does not here suggest that one should have no concern for the things of this world. The KJV mistranslation reads, "Take no thought for your life. . . ." The more sensible, but in many ways more difficult, calling for Christians is to take the proper care for material things, but not to be overly concerned or anxious. We pray, "Give us this day our daily bread" (Matt. 6:11); we do our daily work and make our plans, yet while trusting in God in such a way that we do not let anxiety, insecurity, and greed dominate our individual, family, or community lives. Churches, institutions, and governments can be at least as anxious and greedy as individuals, if not more so.

It is interesting that the English word "anxiety" derives from a Latin root that signifies "narrowness" (hence also our word "angle"). Anxiety comes from and leads to a constriction of vision, trust, openness, and sharing. One remembers that it is "the cares of the world and delight in riches" that "*choke* the word" of God in the interpretation of the parable of the sower (Matt. 13:22). "The Gentiles" who seek after these things (v. 32) here represent all who do not know and trust God and instead live in the service of mammon and in anxiety.

The passage closes on a realistic and somber note. One can plan for tomorrow, but being anxious about it will do no good. Yes, trouble will come, today and tomorrow, but there is only so much one can do about it. Trust in God and put God's reign first.

T. S. Eliot's poem "Ash Wednesday" contains this short petition, "Teach us to care and not to care." His point is not that we are sometimes to care and at other times to be careless. Rather, it is the prayer that we may at once properly care for this world, ourselves, and those in need while at the same time being without care because our ultimate trust is in God. Indeed, that trust is meant to enable Christians to go on caring when life seems to others most hopeless and beyond care. A careless caring and a caring carelessness are intended to be hallmarks of Christians in the world.

The Transfiguration of Our Lord
The Last Sunday after the Epiphany

Lutheran	Roman Catholic	Episcopal	Common Lectionary
Exod. 24:12, 15–18	Dan. 7:9–10, 13–14	Exod. 24:15–18	Exod. 24:12–18
2 Pet. 1:16–19	2 Pet. 1:16–19	Phil. 3:7–14	2 Pet. 1:16–21
Matt. 17:1–9	Matt. 17:1–9	Matt. 17:1–9	Matt. 17:1–9

GOSPEL: MATTHEW 17:1–9

The Sundays of the Epiphany season begin with the baptism of Jesus and end with his transfiguration. In historical, literary, and theological ways these are companion stories with several parallel and echoing features. Together they frame and focus the light of Epiphany glory and mission on the known, yet mysterious, figure of Jesus. He is the human one who was "made like his own people in every respect" (Heb. 2:17) and yet is also the "beloved Son" who once shone before his disciples with the glory light of God.

New Testament scholarship can tell us much about the two narratives, but it cannot finally comprehend their origin or their full significance. Over the past seventy years or so scholars have tended rather loosely to categorize the stories as myths and to see them largely as compositions of the post-resurrection communities, built up for the most part from various pieces of lore drawn from the Hebrew Scriptures. In the case of the transfiguration, Exod. 24:15–18 (with its mountain, cloud, "glory of the Lord like a devouring fire," the presence of Moses and God calling to Moses, and the six days leading to the seventh day) is viewed as the major contributor to the scene. The shining face of Moses (Exod. 34:29–35; see 2 Cor. 3:7–18) and the glory cloud of Exod. 40:34–35 are other motifs which may have been of influence. Jesus is the new Moses (see Deut. 18:15), indeed, the one who surpasses Moses in glory and in God's plan of salvation. Not only does Jesus fulfill the dreams and prophecies of Judaism; they may be said to be fulfilled in him.

Perhaps at some later point the figure of Elijah was added to the story, probably with the idea that, as Moses represented the giving of the law, Elijah was representative of the prophetic tradition. The law and the prophets witnessed to Jesus' glory. Elijah's presence brought another dimension to the narrative—one perhaps already implicit. The last words of the last prophetic book of the Hebrew Scriptures foretell, "Behold, I will send

you Elijah the prophet before the great and terrible day of the Lord comes
. . ." (Mal. 4:5). This prophecy had, of course, impacted the Gospel
tradition in other ways and was linked with the teaching about the Son of
man (see e.g., Matt. 17:9–13; 16:13–14). Elijah's presence adds an eschatological dimension to the transfiguration scene, and some scholars
have interpreted the story as primarily a prefigurement of the Parousia or
coming of Jesus in glory at the end of time.

Sometimes this interpretation is augmented by seeing in the story the
influence of Daniel's powerful image of "the one like a son of man"
coming "with the clouds of heaven" "to the Ancient of Days" (Dan.
7:13). In Dan. 10:5–9 Daniel encounters this son of man—a figure whose
"body was like beryl, his face like the appearance of lightning, his eyes
like flaming torches, his arms and legs like the gleam of burnished bronze,
and the sound of his words like the noise of a multitude," a description
not unlike that in Rev. 1:13–15 of "one like a son of man, clothed with
a long robe and with a golden girdle round his breast; his head and his
hair were white as wool, white as snow; his eyes were like a flame of fire,
his feet were like burnished bronze, refined as in a furnace, and his voice
was like the sound of many waters. . . ." Common and similar features
in the transfiguration story, together with discussion of the mission and
destiny of the Son of man just before and after the transfiguration in the
Synoptic Gospels, have led some interpreters to describe the scene as the
epiphany or transfiguration of the Son of man. Since many in the early
church fervently awaited Jesus' return as "the Son of man coming in clouds
with great power and glory" (Mark 13:26; Matt. 24:30; Luke 21:27; and
see Mark 14:62; Matt. 26:64; Luke 22:69), they understandably would
have been inclined to hear the transfiguration story as an anticipation of
this final Parousia.

Another reason for the presence of Moses and Elijah in the narrative
may be the traditions that they were taken up into heaven (2 Kings 2:1–
12 for Elijah; Moses' ascension was probably described in the lost "As-
sumption of Moses"). In visionary terms, on a high mountain oversha-
dowed by a cloud, this scene takes place in heaven as much as on earth.
It can be viewed as a prefigurement of Jesus' own ascension and glory.

The words of God seem to be drawn mostly from Isa. 42:1 (see The
First Sunday After the Epiphany) and the royal oracle of Ps. 2:7. The
powerful command, "Listen to him," is added to reinforce Jesus' authority
and his teaching as God's Son and the fulfiller of the law and the prophets.

Scholars generally find the booths harder to explain. In narrative terms
they serve as potential places of dwelling for Jesus, Moses, and Elijah—
as though the moment might be extended. Most scholars associate the
booths with the Feast of Booths or Tabernacles, which was then regarded

as the most important of the three major Jewish feasts and had become linked with the tradition of the giving of the law. This association does not, however, seem fully to explain the function of the booths in the story. Other features may also have been added over time. The fear of the disciples (evidently transferred by Matthew from its Markan location in connection with Peter's words to the disciples' response to the voice of God) is an important theme in Mark's presentation of the first disciples of Jesus. They were often fearful of and had trouble understanding the full implications of his ministry. But fear and awe are also regularly a response to theophanies and could well have been an integral part of the narrative. The Greek word *metamorphoō* (see also 2 Cor. 3:18; translated in the Latin by *transfiguratus*) is a more Hellenistic interpretation of the probably earlier Semitic picture of the glory light of divinity shining upon and irradiating the appearance of Jesus.

Although it is now impossible to reach back through the narrative in historical terms, some scholars allow for the possibility that at the heart of the story lay an incident (an experience of Jesus, or of his disciples, or both) in which God's presence was powerfully perceived. But many of the features were added to the narrative over time to express the church's complex and exalted faith in Jesus as the new Moses, the Son of man, and the Servant and Son of God in fulfillment of Isa. 42:1 and Ps. 2:7.

A minority of scholars, myself included, interpret the origin and development of the story rather differently. Noticing that some of the components of the narrative are not well integrated into the scene, and that many of the basic features (cloud, mountain, seven days, shining appearance, voice of God, booths) belong to a widespread mythic and cultic background, we are inclined to see here a story the church has adapted rather than composed—a scene that in some ways was mysterious to them with respect to its origin and full significance. This background, varied in several Middle Eastern cultures and evidenced in partial ways in Jewish lore, centers around the royal cultus and the conception of the king as a kind of representative of the first man. Threatened by but then victorious over the forces of chaos, he is adopted or recognized by the divinity and rules in splendor on the mountain of paradise. Even in the time of Jesus real kings enacted this last part of the ritual by making appearances or epiphanies. Josephus (*Antiquities* 19.8.2) more fully described the scene mentioned in Acts 12:20–23:

> Clad in a garment woven completely of silver so that its texture was indeed wondrous, he [Herod] entered the theater at daybreak. There the silver, illumined by the touch of the first rays of the sun, was wondrously radiant. . . . Straightway his flatterers raised their voices . . . addressing him as a god.

The six and seven days of the Gospels' transfiguration story refer to the creation myth. The booths indicate that it is the Feast of Tabernacles, a traditional time for praying that the creation be restored and for the enthroning of kings.

Both the baptism and transfiguration stories emerge from this heritage, their association with Jesus probably coming through the baptizing sectarian movement in the Jordan valley which, I have argued elsewhere, practiced forms of such rites. Rather than being largely the formation of the post-resurrection church, the narratives would then be later interpretations of earlier tradition.

However we account for the transfiguration in historical terms, its rich theological purpose is to attest to Jesus as the fulfillment of prophecy and the beloved Son of God whose transfiguration offers a glimpse of the glory in which he will one day be known. This mysterious scene, vividly sketched in chiaroscuro, a story that both hides and reveals God's presence, is an invitation to meditate on the faith that Jesus' human life was also a life in which God was present. "He reflects the glory of God and bears the very stamp of God's nature," wrote the author of the Letter to the Hebrews (1:3). Future disciples are meant to perceive this divine light through their faith in the Christ. "It is the God who said, 'Let light shine out of darkness,' who has shone in our hearts to give the light of the knowledge of the glory of God in the face of Christ" (2 Cor. 4:6).

There are many ways to approach the faith that Jesus was a human being who uniquely and decisively expressed the character of God. One way is to start with the biblical insight that all humanity is created in the image of God (Gen. 1:27). Every person is potentially a revelation of God. In Jesus' life, death, and new life that potential was fully realized. Through his human person, the will and nature of God were glimpsed. God could never be known fully. A human life cannot be a complete disclosure, so that the Jesus of history always points beyond himself to God.

It is part of the mystery of this revelation that God's presence in Jesus' life must be perceived more in lowliness and passion than in power and glory. The light of the transfiguration scene is surrounded by dark predictions of suffering and death (Matt. 16:21–25; 17:9). The vision cannot even be told to others until "the Son of man is raised from the dead." Not until the crucifixion has taken place can the character and purpose of God's presence in Jesus' life begin to be understood. Three days from this Sunday Lent begins.

FIRST LESSON: EXODUS 24:12–18

The two other readings for this Sunday, while interesting and useful in their own right, are intended to prepare for the transfiguration story. We have already seen much of the significance of Exod. 24:12–18 in this regard. It, too, is an awesome theophany. While making use of older elements, it is a composition of the so-called priestly authorship that, largely during the exile, gave much of the final character to the Pentateuch. This passage is a kind of narrative bridge between the description of the covenant code and its ratification and the revelation of the tabernacle, its appurtenances, priestly garb, services, and related matters. This detailed presentation continues until chap. 32 when the narrative resumes with the story of the golden calf and the breaking of the covenant. (Exodus 24:12–14 was probably once an introduction to the narrative, a separate tradition about the giving of the Ten Commandments, although chronologically it belongs before chap. 20.)

The mountain is, of course, frequently a locale for a revelation. The six days of v. 16 recall the time of creation. It is on the seventh and culminating day that the glory of the Lord appears and God gives the law, although this is not specifically stated in vv. 16–18 because the priestly author is more interested in the revelations about the tabernacle which will be given during the forty days and nights.

It is significant that here as elsewhere in the Hebrew Scriptures God is heard but not seen. The glory of the Lord signifies the Lord's presence (compare ''the appearance of the likeness of the glory of the Lord'' in Ezek. 1:28), but Israel knows God's words, not God's features. Also in the transfiguration story the Lord is heard and God's presence is visually experienced, but God is not seen. Yet now in the humanity of the transfigured Jesus the character of God shines.

EPISTLE: 2 PETER 1:16–21

The Second Epistle of Peter was written by a later disciple sometime between A.D. 100–150. This form of pseudonymity was an accepted practice of the time for someone who wanted to say, ''This is what Peter would tell us were he alive today.'' The letter has two major purposes, both of which are evident in our passage. First, the author wanted to bolster faith in the second coming of Jesus. Second, he wanted to warn against false prophecy and interpretation of Scripture. The brief description of the transfiguration (vv. 17–18) is useful in both regards. It describes the glory Jesus received during his lifetime, indicative of the favor he has with God. The reference to ''the power and coming (Parousia) of our Lord Jesus Christ,'' though perhaps pointing to the second coming, is probably meant to describe what he showed in his first coming, which helps to guarantee his power to come again in glory.

As a witness to the transfiguration the author is also able to tell the recipients of this letter how the prophetic word of Scripture is to be interpreted. It is not done by individuals acting on their initiative alone. Just as the original writers were moved by the Spirit so must its interpreters today be moved. As presented by apostolic witness the transfiguration becomes "a confirmation of what prophecies have said" (v. 19) enabling them (in a lovely image) to be like a lamp "until the day *(hēmera,* with eschatological nuances of the day of the Lord) dawns and the morning star *(phōsphoros,* or "light bringer," Venus) arises and illuminates your minds"—until the coming of Christ either in fullness or by the light of revelation.

This passage begins with an assurance that Petrine tradition did not follow "cleverly devised myths." Yet New Testament scholarship often classifies the transfiguration as a "myth" and outsiders to Christianity might view it as only "devised" or "invented." The power of faithful preaching is called upon to help congregations see the truth to which these words and images and the use of ancient prophecy all seek to point. In ways that finally go beyond the capacity of words to tell, the glory of the infinite God, Creator of the heavens and every world, was present in the human life of Jesus, the Christ.